Battle Orders · 15

German Airborne Divisions: Mediterranean Theatre 1942–45

Fig. 9: 1 Fallschirmjäger Division at Cassino, 11–22 May 1944 (artillery excluded)

Bruce Quarrie · *Consultant editor Dr Duncan Anderson*

Series editors Marcus Cowper and Nikolai Bogdanovic

First published in 2005 by Osprey Publishing
Midland House, West Way, Botley, Oxford OX2 0PH, UK
443 Park Avenue South, New York, NY 10016, USA
E-mail: info@ospreypublishing.com

A CIP catalogue record for this book is available from the British Library

ISBN 1 84176 828 6

Consultant editor: Duncan Anderson
Editorial by Ilios Publishing, Oxford, UK (www.iliospublishing.com)
Page layouts by Bounford.com, Royston, UK
Index by Sandra Shotter
Maps by Bounford.com, Royston, UK

Originated by The Electronic Page Company, Cwmbran, UK
Printed in China through Bookbuilders.

05 06 07 08 09   10 9 8 7 6 5 4 3 2 1

For a catalogue of all books published by Osprey Military and Aviation please contact:
NORTH AMERICA
Osprey Direct, 2427 Bond Street, University Park, IL 60466, USA
E-mail: info@ospreydirectusa.com

ALL OTHER REGIONS
Osprey Direct UK, P.O. Box 140 Wellingborough, Northants, NN8 2FA, UK
E-mail: info@ospreydirect.co.uk

www.ospreypublishing.com

Acknowledgements

To Pier Paolo Battistelli for unstinting help from his university
research into Il Paracadutisti; and to Mike Holm for much obscure
information about flying units. Any errors in 'downloading' the
data are entirely my own.

Editor's note

As this was the last book Bruce was working on before he lost
the battle to lung cancer on 4 September 2004, his wife and
children would like to thank everyone who was involved in
making the publication possible. He would have been pleased
and proud that his work ended in print.
In particular, I would like to thank Pier Paolo Battistelli, without
whose expert help with the unit trees, maps, text and photos,
this book would never have been completed. I would also like
to thank Lieutenant-Colonel Filippo Cappellano, Dottor Pier
Crociani and Count Ernesto G. Vitetti for their help in providing
photographs and captions.

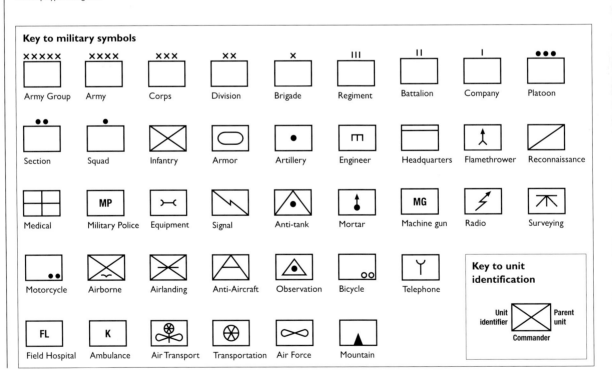

Key to military symbols

xxxxx	Army Group
xxxx	Army
xxx	Corps
xx	Division
x	Brigade
III	Regiment
II	Battalion
I	Company
•••	Platoon
••	Section
•	Squad
⊠	Infantry
⬭	Armor
•	Artillery
⊓	Engineer
	Headquarters
⟑	Flamethrower
⟋	Reconnaissance
	Medical
MP	Military Police
⊢⊣	Equipment
⟋	Signal
▲	Anti-tank
↑	Mortar
MG	Machine gun
⚡	Radio
⟑	Surveying
••	Motorcycle
⊠	Airborne
⊠	Airlanding
▲	Anti-Aircraft
▲	Observation
oo	Bicycle
Y	Telephone
FL	Field Hospital
K	Ambulance
✹	Air Transport
⊕	Transportation
∞	Air Force
▲	Mountain

Key to unit identification

Unit identifier — Commander — Parent unit

Contents

Introduction

The ten-day battle for Crete in May 1941 was a watershed in the annals of airborne forces worldwide, being the first time in history that almost an entire division of men was dropped to secure a major strategic target. Prior to this, in April–June 1940 the Fallschirmjäger had only been used in relatively small battlegroups to seize tactical objectives. The early operations were, overall, spectacularly successful though; so much so, in fact, that during the remainder of that summer English villagers daily anticipated swarms of German paratroopers leaping upon them, and sharpened their pitchforks. Gradually, however, with the Luftwaffe's failure to beat the Royal Air Force into submission during the Battle of Britain, such apprehensions faded – but Polish and Czech fighter pilots forced to bale out continued to receive rough handling until they managed to establish their identities. Fears of 'fifth columnists' were also rife, and all adults of known German extraction living in Britain were subjected to rigorous screening. Many of them, including a large number of Jews who had sought asylum from Nazi persecution, were placed in internment centres, while all those whom Winston Churchill called 'doubtful elements' who lived within five miles of the coast were forcibly relocated inland.

It was in this paranoiac environment that, as early as 6 June 1940, Churchill astonishingly proposed the 'deployment of [British] parachute troops on a scale equal to 5,000'. Even while the forces sent to Norway were still being shipped home from Narvik following the earlier evacuation from Dunkirk, he was already thinking of an eventual comeback, and the fortuitous capture of

General Kurt Student inspecting paratroopers somewhere in the Mediterranean theatre.

a Fallschirmjäger field manual by Dutch troops at Ypenburg provided much food for thought. In Germany of course the paratroops' exploits, hyped by Goebbels' propaganda machine, produced a rush of volunteers and a political climate that allowed Reichsmarschall Hermann Göring to begin a further expansion of his Fallschirmkorps. However, this was initially limited because the OKW refused to accept his proposal for the urgent creation of four more airborne divisions. Similarly, Kurt Student's plan to drop 7 Flieger Division near Folkestone on the south-east coast of England to capture the airfield at Lympne as part of Operation Sëelowe was abandoned when the whole project was put on ice.

The 7 Flieger Division that landed on Crete in May 1941 was nevertheless a far cry from its 1940 counterpart, numerically stronger and better equipped. Despite this, the invasion of the island nearly failed and the casualties were so heavy that Hitler asserted 'the day of the paratrooper is over'. In England, however, where only the German success was seen rather than its cost, the lessons of Crete further accelerated development of what would become the 1st and 6th Airborne Divisions, as well as a variety of other airborne and airlanding formations. This was the 'watershed'. Germany virtually turned its back on paratroops while Britain – not to mention Italy, and the United States after Pearl Harbor six months later – desired only to expand their potential.

Up to this point 7 Flieger Division, as an air force formation, had operated under the aegis of the Oberkommando der Luftwaffe (OKL). The two army divisions assigned to its support – 22 Infanterie Division (Luftlande) in 1940 and 5 Gebirgsjäger Division in 1941 – similarly came under temporary air force control. From now on, however, the airborne forces would instead be subordinated to Oberkommando des Heeres (OKH) operational requirements. The parachute division created since 1938 with so much enthusiasm and effort was therefore despatched in 'penny packets' to the Eastern Front as ordinary infantry after its regiments had been partially rebuilt in the wake of Crete. Here, they again suffered so many casualties that they were withdrawn after only a few weeks, apart from two Kampfgruppen that continued fighting in the east for several months. Next, plans to use a composite brigade together with an Italian parachute and airlanding division for an invasion of Malta were also abandoned and the troops earmarked for this despatched to North Africa instead, so the year 1942 effectively saw the paras frittered away as ersatz or replacement formations rather than as the spearpoint.

However, this was far from the end of the Fallschirmkorps because Hermann Göring and his protégé, General der Flieger Kurt Student, along with a number of other high-ranking and influential officers, retained confidence in their men's capabilities and in a resurrection of the Führer's earlier enthusiasm. The latter was partially rekindled by the Anglo-American use of paratroops in North Africa following Operation Torch in November 1942, and the year 1943 finally saw the beginning of the creation of the four new airborne divisions Göring had wanted, resulting in 7 Flieger Division being renamed 1 Fallschirmjäger Division in May. The number of parachute training schools was also increased and XI Fliegerkorps was replaced by I and II Fallschirmkorps in Italy and France respectively. However, by this time Germany was fighting a defensive war on all fronts so, despite this expansion, Göring and Student were still unable to persuade Hitler or the OKW to allow them to conduct more than a handful of small airborne operations. On Sunday, 17 September 1944, Student's frustration expressed itself clearly when, watching the parachutes of the American 101st Airborne Division descend around Eindhoven during Operation Market Garden, he asked a staff officer wistfully, 'What might I have accomplished had I such a force at my disposal?'

Combat mission

Student's *cri de coeur* was echoed by many in the Fallschirmtruppe after Crete. Were all the hard work and careful planning of the previous three years, plus the ongoing development of new weapons and equipment, simply to be thrown away? Were they going to have to abandon their beloved Ju 52s for pedestrian trains and trucks? What battlefield function was left to them?

Alongside Student, the majority of men in the Fallschirmkorps firmly believed that the paratroop role itself was still viable. After all, they reasoned, even though it had been difficult to get the corps established in the first place, battling against entrenched scepticism, they had since proved that they could win other battles in the face of adversity and superior numbers. This combat experience could surely not be disregarded? For the time being, though, in June 1941 with the panzers streaming into Russia, all they could do was listen to the news on radio and wish they were there to help. They looked at maps and saw that the Soviet Union was bisected by great rivers that predominantly ran north and south, against the grain of the assault. Capturing bridges to speed the tanks' progress was one of the combat missions the airborne corps had been specifically created to achieve. The maps also revealed the vast distances

General Ramcke, his exact rank at this date obscured in this photo, decorates a paratrooper NCO somewhere in the Mediterranean theatre.

involved that were already hindering the Luftwaffe in maintaining support along the rapidly moving front lines. Capturing forward airfields so that the bombers and fighters could rearm, refuel and return to the battlefield more quickly was another Fallschirmjäger speciality. Why, the men asked, were they not called upon? Why could the planners at OKW not see the obvious?

All their arguments ran into the brick wall of Hitler's obstinacy. He had suffered grave misgivings about the airborne invasion of Crete in the first place, and the paras' subsequent losses reinforced his belief in his own infallibility. Any plans Kurt Student submitted to OKW were peremptorily dismissed. The men of 7 Flieger Division itself, now with Generalleutnant[1] Erich Petersen as CO following Wilhelm Süßmann's death en route to Crete, licked their wounds, drank to their lost comrades and idled the hot summer of 1941 away while their ranks were refilled by nervous but enthusiastic new recruits (Fig. 1, page 20). Then at last in September came the news that some of them at least were to be sent to Russia after all, even though it was by train. Here, on the northern front, the inexperience and comparative lack of training amongst the replacements showed itself in further severe losses and most of the shaken but still not demoralized survivors were pulled out of the line in November/December while OKW debated their fate once more.

By early 1942, the invasion of Russia was already faltering with German armies largely dug into static lines in front of Leningrad and Moscow. Only in the south did there seem to be any opportunity for a new blitzkrieg. Here, the wide-open steppes with their rich grainfields and the lure of the distant oilfields of the Caucasus beckoned, along with the symbolic city of Stalingrad. Oil, or rather the lack of it, was already of increasing concern in Germany, and Hitler did momentarily toy with the idea of using the Fallschirmjäger to seize the Black Sea refinery port at Batum, taking off from captured airfields in the Crimea. However, even he saw that this would have been a suicide mission with prompt relief by ground forces impossible to guarantee, so his fertile but erratic imagination wandered even further afield.

In North Africa, Erwin Rommel had also been temporarily forced on to the defensive at the end of 1941, fought to a standstill at Sidi Rezegh and unable to take Tobruk. In order to capture Egypt and then potentially sweep north into pro-Axis Syria and Iraq with their own precious oilfields, he urgently needed reinforcements in men and *matériel*. Both were in short supply because of the demands of the Russian front, beside which, with the Italian navy's demoralising defeats at Taranto and Matapan in 1940 and 1941, the Royal Navy virtually dominated his Mediterranean convoy routes. The key to safeguarding them seemed to be another island even more pivotal than Crete: Malta.

The original idea for an invasion of Malta seems, however, to have been Mussolini's. He had been infuriated in April/May 1940 when Hitler moved into Scandinavia and western Europe without consulting or even telling him, and his own invasion of Greece that October was a deliberate rebuke to his fellow dictator. When this as well as the practically simultaneous invasion of Egypt failed disastrously, necessitating German intervention on both fronts, Mussolini was desperate to regain military credibility. The fact that Italian troops did contribute, however marginally, to the victory on Crete probably spurred his imagination, and in August 1941 he authorized the formation of a parachute division, followed two months later by an airlanding division. To Il Duce's chagrin, though, when Feldmarschall Albert Kesselring was appointed Oberbefehlshaber Süd in December and nominally put in charge of all Axis troops in the Mediterranean theatre, he took control of the Italian plan. With Kurt Student appointed as commander of the airborne and airlanding side of the mission, it then began taking revised shape as Operation Herkules, in which the rump of 7 Flieger Division would, it was intended, have a critical combat role as 'stiffening' for the Italian forces that were numerically far stronger. The Regia Marina would be forced to play its reluctant part, promised massive air cover by Regia Aeronautica and Luftwaffe squadrons based in southern Italy and on Sicily that would hopefully keep the Royal Navy at bay. (Despite its earlier successes at sea, the RN had begun to learn what land-based air power could achieve in the waters around Crete, which were dubbed 'bomb alley'. If the German paras had suffered badly during Operation Merkur, the RN had not fared much better with nine ships lost and 1,828 dead.)

While planning continued, Student despatched German instructors to help whip the Italian assault troops into fighting trim, and in April Generalmajor Bernhard Ramcke was given command of a new 1 Fallschirmjäger Brigade (Fig. 2, page 26). Although most of the paras were eager and even the Italian Commando Supremo motivated by the thought of removing this thorn from its flesh, Hitler vacillated as he had done before Crete. Surprisingly, it was effectively Hermann Göring – the creator of the Fallschirmtruppe – who caused the plan to be aborted because, he claimed, the Luftwaffe could pulverize the Maltese defenders into submission on its own. Ignoring Kesselring's justifiable objection that the Luftwaffe lacked the strategic bombing capability to achieve this miracle, Hitler listened to his Reichsmarschall instead and, to the mixed disappointment and relief of the troops who would have been involved, the whole mission was shelved. Ramcke's brigade, followed by the bulk of the Italian 'Folgore' Parachute Division (Fig. 12, page 56), was therefore despatched to Egypt because Rommel had finally succeeded in capturing Tobruk anyway and brought the Afrika Korps within striking distance of the Suez Canal.

German operational doctrine in the early war years relied heavily on reinforcing success rather than bolstering failure, so Rommel appreciated the arrival of Ramcke's tough Fallschirmjäger in particular, even though a single brigade was numerically insignificant amongst the eight Italian divisions (nine including the Blackshirts) and four German (five including the Flak) plus the

A mixed group of German and Italian paratroopers at Anzio in February 1944. The German Fallschirmjäger in the centre displays the front pocket detail of the jump trousers, the two Italian paratroopers to the right wear smocks made from Italian Army camouflage material.

assorted other regiments and battalions already in North Africa. 'Folgore' was also welcome, but it was untried in battle and Rommel distrusted Italian troops with some justification, despite the fact that in truth it was usually ineptitude, sloth and corruption in the officer corps rather than any lack of courage amongst the front-line soldiers that gave the Italian forces of World War II their poor reputation. Rommel also asked for 22 Luftlande Division, now renamed Tropisch, which was fully motorized with armoured cars, self-propelled Flak and towed rather than horse-drawn artillery, to be released to him. Kesselring, who disliked Rommel intensely for reasons discussed later, and was out of countenance anyway by the dismissal of the Maltese plan, found excuses for refusal, and apart from a single battalion (III/IR 47), the division that might have made a significant difference during the impending battles around Alam Halfa and El Alamein was wasted as a fortress garrison on Crete.

The Ramcke Brigade's deployment to Africa, following those of Kampfgruppen 'Meindl' and 'Sturm' earlier to Russia, effectively marked the beginning of what, for the most part, would become the primary Fallschirmjäger combat mission for the remainder of the war. It is axiomatic that the best form of defence is offence. If you can also attack from an unexpected direction, which the paras specialized in, then the other old adage that 'the bigger they are, the harder they fall' is likely to be equally true. Unfortunately for the paras, at Alamein they were denied any advantage of surprise while God at this time was on the side of Montgomery's 'big battalions' and Ramcke was very lucky to escape with as much of his command intact as he did.

Further Fallschirmjäger deployments in the Mediterranean theatre represented another new mission for the paras that, in business terms, might have been called 'crisis management'. An example of this is the resurrection of a contingency plan drawn up by Student in December 1940 to use a combined glider and parachute force to seize the Mediterranean port of Toulon in case the French Fleet tried to defect. This plan was hastily dusted off in the wake of Operation Torch, and FJR 5 – two battalions of which were already in the south of France – was briefly considered for the assignment. In the event, the French navy made no attempt to move and the regiment was sent to Tunisia instead to help try to manage another crisis (Fig. 4, page 29).

Hence also the subsequent deployments of 1 and (briefly) 2 Fallschirmjäger Divisions to Sicily and Italy in the summer of 1943, and the creation of 4 Fallschirmjäger Division (Fig. 8, page 41) after the Italian surrender. Here the paras were reunited alongside the Fallschirm-Panzer Division 'Hermann Göring', whose original 'General Göring' Regiment had given birth to the airborne corps in 1936. As in Africa and on other fronts, the paratroops were comparatively few in numbers in Italy (see panel) but more than made up for this through skill and determination. As in Russia, the Fallschirmjäger had now become an elite rapid reaction force, a 'fire brigade', much as the principal Waffen-SS formations were. Ironically, however, there was also a return to the earliest days of the airborne concept and they were used as reconnaissance and pathfinder teams as well as in several small-scale and almost police-style missions described later. Despite all this, their combat potential was effectively wasted, as Kurt Student saw so clearly.

German divisions on the Italian front 1943–45
A total of 33 Wehrmacht and four Waffen-SS divisions were deployed on Sicily, Sardinia and the mainland for varying periods from a few days to two years: 1, 2 and 4 Fallschirmjäger; 5 and 188 Gebirgsjäger, plus 24 SS; 42 and 114 Jäger; 34, 44, 65, 71, 76, 92, 94, 98, 148, 155 Feldersatz, 162, 232, 237, 278, 305, 334, 356, 362, 710 and 715 Infanterie, plus 29 SS-Grenadier; 3, 15, 29 and 90 Panzergrenadier plus 16 SS; 16 and 26 Panzer, plus 'Hermann Göring' and 1 SS; and 19 and 20 Luftwaffen-Feld.

Preparation for war: doctrine and training

By 1942 the Fallschirmjäger had already been at war on several fronts for over two years so it was only novices who needed any 'preparation'. They had a solid nucleus of veterans who included some of the best tactical instructors in the entire Wehrmacht and who drove home their hard-earned lessons. The only real changes in training since the blitzkrieg era were that the number of qualifying jumps was reduced from six to four, and a progressively greater emphasis was placed on defensive stratagems. There was, of course, also induction in the use of all the new equipment that was introduced during 1942–45.

Parachute training itself was decentralized from Stendal to accommodate the expected growth in volunteers when the four planned new divisions began slowly taking shape. The resulting changes were more than a little confusing because of renumbering and moves to different locations. First, the original Luftwaffe school at Stendal-Borstel was relocated to Wittstock-Dosse in December 1942 to make room for a new 2 Fallschirmschule. Within days this had been moved to Braunschweig-Broitzen, home of the army's prewar school, but it was disbanded at the beginning of 1943; 1 Fallschirmschule at Wittstock was then renumbered 2. Meanwhile, 3 Fallschirmschule was brought into existence at Braunschweig before moving to Kraljevo in Serbia early in 1943. Over the same short period, 4 Fallschirmschule was formed at Dreux in France before being renumbered 1 a year later, when it then absorbed the personnel of No. 2 (the original No. 1). It was finally dissolved on 20 August 1944, most of its personnel forming the Greve Fallschirmjäger-Ersatz Regiment that in turn became III/FJR 21 as part of 7 Fallschirmjäger Division on 25 November. Finally, the remaining instructors from the earlier 4 Fallschirmschule were moved to Freiburg-Salzwedel to become the very last 1 Fallschirmschule! When a Kommando der Fallschirmjäger-Schulen was belatedly created at Berlin-Tempelhof in January 1945, Salzwedel became responsible for NCO training with a leadership school at Goslar. Throughout all this chaos, it is unremarkable that a true paratroop capability was only really retained in 1 and 2 Fallschirmjäger Divisions; comparatively few men in the higher numbered divisions were entitled to wear the coveted jump badge, other than cadres from the parent formations.

Nevertheless, 'The secret of the paratroops' success can be summed up in three words: comradeship, esprit de corps and efficiency'. So wrote Major Rudolf Böhmler, CO of I/FJR 3, in the aftermath of the battles for Cassino. The question is, how did the Fallschirmjäger manage to retain these qualities when so many men were becoming disillusioned by the loss of their primary role? Re-examination of Hitler's prewar 'Ten Commandments to the Paratroops' provides a partial clue. The following is something of a 'free' translation:

1. You are the first chosen of the German army.
2. You will seek combat and train to endure every ordeal.
3. Battle shall be your sole fulfilment.
4. Care for your comrades because it is by their help that you will triumph or die.
5. Watch your words. They are not incorruptible. Men act while women gossip. Loose talk can bring you to your grave.
6. Be calm and careful, strong and decisive. Courage and enthusiasm will give you the upper hand in the attack.

7. Your best friend in the face of the enemy is your ammunition. Those who shoot aimlessly to calm themselves down do not deserve the name paratroopers.
8. You can only be victorious when your weapons are good. You must hold fast to them: 'First my weapons, then myself'.
9. You must understand each mission fully, so that if your leader falls you can carry on by yourself. Fight against an open foe with chivalry, but extend no quarter to a partisan.
10. Keep your eyes open, be swift as a greyhound, tough as leather, hard as Krupp steel, and in this way you will become the embodiment of the German warrior.

Much of this is pure common sense mixed with rhetoric and in the nature of a 'pep talk'. The obvious ingredients of the doctrine are well known to any soldier and endlessly rehearsed during training. Aggression not hesitancy wins battles, make sure you know the mission profile so that you can carry on when things go wrong (since no battle plan ever survives the first encounter), keep yourself physically fit and mentally alert, look after your friends and they will look after you, care for your weapons and don't waste ammunition. 'Careless talk costs lives' or its equivalent was a propaganda slogan in every country after 1939 and its inclusion in the 'commandments' seems rather unnecessary, but more to the point, why did Hitler then go on to select guerrillas for special attention? Did he somehow guess at such an early stage that the resistance movements in the occupied countries were going to prove so much of a drain on manpower and resources? It almost seems prophetic because the Fallschirmjäger certainly encountered plenty of partisan activity on Crete and later in Russia, France, Italy and Yugoslavia.

On 7 October 1942 Hitler went even further in his diatribe against irregular warfare. He was particularly incensed by British Commando hit and run raids, and the Dieppe operation in August had shaken him, so a Wehrmacht Order of the Day (Tagesbefehl) singled out Commandos for summary execution whether they were in uniform or not, armed or not, dropped by parachute or landed by other means, and even if they tried to surrender. Such troops were to be 'ruthlessly mown down wherever they may appear'. Apparently, the Führer had conveniently forgotten that his own 'Brandenburg' Regiment had successfully employed similar Commando-style tactics in Poland, Holland and Russia, including the use of enemy uniforms as a ruse de guerre.

The order provoked outrage amongst many German field commanders and Kesselring and Rommel were in agreement for once, refusing to pass it on to their men. The Fallschirmtruppe were especially concerned because the British and their allies could have retaliated quite reasonably by ordering that all German paratroops were similarly to be executed on sight. In response, five days later Hitler amended his Kommandobefehl with a clause stating that, ' This order does not apply to the treatment of any soldiers who, in the course of normal hostilities, large-scale offensive actions, landing operations and airborne operations, are captured in open battle or give themselves up.'

This 'clarification' only served to muddy the water and led to understandable confusion amongst the men who were expected to carry the orders out. Tangible evidence emerged only a month later and proved that the Fallschirmjäger doctrine was more keyed to the chivalric element of their 'ninth commandment'. On 29 November the British 2nd Parachute Battalion under Major John Frost was dropped at Depienne in Tunisia to secure three airfields in the vicinity. When Depienne itself was found to be abandoned, Frost led his battalion off in search of the other targets, but he had to leave behind those men who had been injured in the drop on to hard, uneven ground, with a single platoon to safeguard them. They were soon discovered by a patrol from Oberstleutnant Walter Koch's freshly arrived I/FJR 5

Depienne, Tunisia, November 1943. Hauptmann Hans Jungwirth of I/FJR 5 (left) with his prisoner, Cpl. Gavin Cadden of the British 2nd Parachute Battalion, 6th Parachute Brigade.

and, although the British platoon put up a gallant fight, it was quickly overwhelmed. Koch had his own medics help tend to the injured and wounded, then left them with food, water and cigarettes before handing them over to regular ground forces, believed to have been from 90 Aufklärungs-Abteilung of 10 Panzer Division. The officer in charge of this unit had read Hitler's original Tagesbefehl and ordered the British paras shot. (One of the survivors later told me he had black insignia, so he may have been an SS or SD officer attached to ensure 'political correctness'.) A machine gun had already been set up when Koch and his I Bataillon CO, Hauptmann Hans Jungwirth, returned as if by a premonition. Koch halted the execution after a heated exchange and demanded that his prisoners be treated properly – which they subsequently were, ending up in POW camps in Italy from which many escaped after the armistice a few months later.

This was the first time that 'Red Devil' had met 'Grün Teufel' in combat, although it would not be the last, and even though this particular story did not emerge until after the war, the incident helped cement the close camaraderie and respect that still exists between German and British paras. There can be few better examples of the doctrine the Fallschirmjäger had adopted for themselves, even without Hitler's 'commandments', which could be summarized in the old adage 'do as you would be done by' even without its cynical addition, 'but do it first'. This demanded self-discipline rather than imposed discipline, a key element reinforced in training alongside self-reliance. The crux of it all was leadership, not from the Führerhauptquartier with its contradictory demands but from individual company, battalion, regiment and division commanders. Here, the men were well served, although there is only room for character sketches of a few.

Command, control, communications and intelligence (C3I)

Walter Koch in many ways epitomizes both the Fallschirmjäger ethos and the quality of leadership that helped give the 'Green Devils' their outstanding combat record and the high regard of all their opponents throughout the war. Born in 1910, he obviously missed service during World War I but joined the Berlin police force in 1929, rising to the rank of Leutnant in Landespolizei-gruppe 'Wecke' and Oberleutnant in 1935 after it was renamed Regiment 'General Göring'. He was one of the early volunteers for the original Fallschirmschützen-Bataillon where he was in good company amongst several other gifted junior and middle level leaders who later distinguished themselves and rose to high positions in the Fallschirmtruppe, not least because of their belief in leading from the front.

After gaining his parachute 'wings' in September 1936, Koch became CO of I/FJR 1 in April 1938 and, promoted to Hauptmann later the same month, also learned to pilot an aircraft. Next year, his ambition, initiative and resourcefulness were put to the test by his selection as leader of the airlanding assault battalion that was to spearhead the attack on Belgium in May 1940 (Sturmabteilung 'Koch'). Success at Eben Emael made him a national hero and gave him further promotion to Major plus a Knight's Cross, along with command of I Bataillon in the enlarged Luftlande-Sturm Regiment under Oberst Eugen Meindl. Both men were wounded on Crete but were reunited in Russia for six months during November 1941–May 1942 before Koch, promoted again to Oberstleutnant, was given command of the new FJR 5 then forming at Reims in France. Moved via Caserta in Italy in November, he and most of his men were airlanded at Tunis over the 12th to the 16th, and a fortnight later met their new adversaries at Depienne. Koch was hospitalized again in February 1943 and after convalescence in Germany was transferred to OKL Reserve. However, his opposition to the Kommandobefehl had not escaped notice and Koch died in a Berlin hospital on 27 October after a mysterious road 'accident' involving an unlit tank transporter. Like Rommel a year later, he had become too much of a media figure to be executed officially. The present-day Fallschirmjäger still lay a wreath on his grave in his home city, Bonn, every October.

Eugen Meindl had a very different career from Koch's that provides a valuable contrast because the two men's stories actually complement each other rather well. Both demonstrate the diversity of talent and the motivation within the leadership of the Fallschirmtruppe that kept the men's morale and combat capability so high right to the bitter end. Born in Donaueschingen, Austria, in 1892, Meindl was commissioned into the Austro-Hungarian army in 1912, seeing service throughout World War I as an artillery battery commander. During the interwar years he rose through the ranks in Artillerie Regiment Nr.5 to Major in 1934 but demanded fresh challenge and, after the Anschluß, in November 1938 with the rank of Oberstleutnant he became Chef of Artillerie Regiment Nr.112 in Generalmajor Eduard Dietl's new 3 Gebirgsjäger Division. Meindl's gunners fought on the southern front in Poland practically alongside Oberst Hans Kreysing's Infanterie Regiment Nr.12 from 22 Infanterie Division, which seems irrelevant but forged one of those strange bonds that pervade the whole story of the Fallschirm-und-Gebirgstruppe throughout the war.

General der Fallschirmtruppe Herman-Bernhard Ramcke
1889 Born 24 January, Schleswig
1904–07 With Marine Boys' Division as a Schiffszungen
1907–08 Promoted to Matrose
1908–14 Service aboard various cruisers and battleship *Wettin*
1914–15 War service aboard cruiser *Prinz Adalbert*
1915–16 Platoon leader in Nr. 2 Matrosen Regiment in Flanders; promoted to Feldwebel
1916–17 Wounded, hospitalized for 18 months; promoted to Offizier-Stellvertreter
1917–18 Platoon leader in Marinekorps Sturmabteilung in Flanders; wounded again; promoted to Leutnant
1919 Company commander in Freikorps 'von Brandis'; transferred from Marine to Heer (March); wounded again
1920–35 Various appointments in IR 1, 2 and 3; promotions – Oberleutnant (1921), Hauptmann (1927), Major (1934)
1936–1940 Various staff appointments
1940 Parachute training at Braunschweig (July); Fallschirmschützenabzeichen 1 August; transferred to Luftwaffe and promoted to Oberst same date; Stab, FJR 1
1941 CO of XI Fliegerkorps' operational training schools; simultaneously (21 May–18 June) CO of LLStR on Crete; promoted to Generalmajor (July); Ritterkreuz (August)
1942 Seconded to Regio Esercito (March); CO of 1 Fallschirm Brigade (April); Eichenlaub (August); promoted to Generalleutnant (December)
1943 Began forming 2 Fallschirmjäger Division (February); hospitalized (September)
1944 Returned to duty (February); Kommandeur of 'Festung Brest' (11 August); promoted to General der Fallschirmtruppe 14 September); Schwerten und Brillanten (19 September); surrendered 20 September
1944–46 POW in Britain
1946–51 Imprisoned by French
1951–68 In retirement; died 5 July 1968, Kappeln

General der Fallschirmtruppe Richard Heidrich

1896 Born 29 July, Lewald (Saxony)

1914 Schütze in Infanterie Regiment Nr.101

1915–18 Promoted to Gefreiter in Saxon IR 3 then Feldwebel in IR 102 then field commission to Leutnant in Saxon IR 16 – the regiment that later formed the nucleus for 22 Luftlande Division; wounded on the Somme

1919 Joined Freikorps 'von Brandis' alongside Ramcke

1920–24 Postings unknown

1925 Promoted to Oberleutnant; instructor at the Dresden Infanterieschule

1931 Promoted to Hauptmann; put in charge of all NCO training at Dresden

1934–38 Lecturer in tactics at the Dresden, Munich and Potsdam Infantry Schools; promoted to Major (1937); Fallschirmschützenabzeichen 12 October 1937

1938 Appointed CO of Fallschirm-Infanterie-Bataillon des Heeres (June)

1939 Transferred to Luftwaffe (January); promoted to Oberstleutnant; CO of FJR 2 (August)

1939–40 Seconded back to OKH; CO of Infanterie-Ersatz Regiment Nr. 4 (December–February); CO of Saxon IR 514, 294 Infanterie Division (March–May); promoted to Oberst (April); reverted to Luftwaffe; CO of FJR 3 (from 31 May)

1941 CO of Gruppe Mitte on Crete after Wilhelm Süßmann's death; Ritterkreuz (June)

1942 Promoted to Generalmajor as CO of 7 Flieger Division (1 August)

1943 CO of 1 Fallschirmjäger Division (1 May); promoted to Generalleutnant (July)

1944 Eichenlaub (February); Schwerten (March); Kommandeur of I Fallschirmkorps (16 September); promoted to General der Fallschirmtruppe (October)

1945 Surrendered to British forces (May)

1947 Released from internment due to illness (July); died in Hamburg 22 December

Kreysing's regiment became part of Kurt Student's Luftlandekorps for the invasion of Holland in 1940, creating the first airborne link, while Kreysing himself became later CO of 3 Gebirgsjäger Division in 1942.

Meanwhile, Meindl had also changed horses. When 3 Gebirgsjäger Division ran into severe difficulties at Narvik in June 1940, and Dietl was even contemplating withdrawing his men into internment in neutral Sweden, Kesselring and Student had Hauptmann Erich Pietzonka's II/FJR 2 dropped to their assistance. Meindl and 200 men from the mountain division who had not so far been involved in the Norwegian campaign volunteered for a 'crash' parachute course and dropped with the battalion. Meindl was so entranced by the experience that in August he arranged a transfer to the Luftwaffe and on 1 September became Colonel of the new Luftlande-Sturm Regiment with Walter Koch an invaluable confidant. After Crete, and service in Russia, Meindl avoided Hitler's purges to become a General der Fallschirmtruppe and CO of II Fallschirmkorps in France a week after Koch's death, on 5 November 1943.

The accompanying panels show further similarities and contrasts between the three principal Fallschirmjäger divisional commanders involved in the Mediterranean campaigns of 1942–45 – different backgrounds, different technical expertise, different ages – but ultimately united in purpose. Here we have a soldier, sailor and airman, but each of them importantly with prewar combat experience and the ability to win the trust and respect of their men. Before rising to divisional command, Heidrich and Ramcke were highly regarded as inspirational instructors who could extract the very best from any group of recruits, while Trettner was so capable an administrator that for a long time he was denied the combat command he so desired. All three proved their leadership qualities in the field as well, though Ramcke became the most highly decorated officer in the wartime Fallschirmtruppe, while Heidrich, who devoted his whole life to soldiering and never married, conducted the defence of Cassino in particular with consummate skill before becoming CO of I Fallschirmkorps. Trettner commanded the mixed bag of German and Italian paras in his own division with diplomacy and earned their loyalty even though he never completed the six necessary qualifying jumps for the Fallschirm-schützenabzeichen. Ironically, perhaps, two of them – Ramcke and Trettner – later shared the same fate as inmates of Special Camp XI, Island Farm, near Bridgend in Wales, from 1946 to 1947 while still under suspicion of possible war crimes. Here they were reunited with Kurt Student himself, Eugen Meindl, Gerhard Bassenge and Alfred Schlemm.

Bassenge, a World War I fighter 'ace', commanded the original jump school at Stendal from 1937 to 1938 before becoming chief of staff for varying periods to Student, Richard Putzier, Kesselring and Hans-Jürgen Stumpff. He was captured on 10 May 1943 while commander of Fortress Area Tunis-Bizerta. Schlemm, like Meindl, had fielded an artillery battery during World War I and held various staff appointments in the Reichsheer before transferring to the Luftwaffe in 1938. He was Student's chief of staff in XI Fliegerkorps from December 1940 to February 1942, then commanded a Kampfgruppe in XL Panzerkorps on the Russian front for three months and 1 Flieger Division for a further three before being given II Luftwaffen-Feld Korps; this was renamed I Fallschirmkorps when its staff was reconstituted in Italy on 1 January 1944. In November he relinquished this post to Heidrich in order to succeed Student as CO of 1 Fallschirm Armee in Holland. Badly wounded during the Allied Rhine crossings, he was captured by the British in May 1945.

One final individual deserves special mention in the 'command' context even though, like Schlemm, Trettner and Student himself, he was never a qualified paratrooper: Albert Kesselring. He was, however, Hitler's choice as C-in-C of all German and Italian ground and air forces in North Africa and Italy from December 1941 to March 1945, including the Fallschirmjäger. This helps set their deployments within the larger strategic context rather then merely tactical. Unfortunately, Kesselring's published memoirs reveal little of the man himself, being more a catalogue of events, so we are largely left to interpret his motives through what his contemporaries said about him. He was born in Bayreuth, Bavaria, in 1885 and joined the army as an ensign (Fahnenjunker) in 1904. Like Meindl and Schlemm, his technical inquisitiveness took him into the artillery and he served as a battery commander on both the Western and Eastern Fronts during World War I. His administrative talents led to his selection for the General Staff in 1917 and five years later General Hans von Seeckt chose him to become, in effect, his chief of staff in the Heeresleitung (see Osprey's Battle Orders 4: *German Airborne Divisions: Blitzkrieg 1940–41* by the same author). In this post, and despite the restrictions of the Treaty of Versailles, Kesselring not only helped streamline the army's cumbersome bureaucratic structure and laid down guidelines for what would eventually emerge as the tri-service Oberkommando der Wehrmacht, but also encouraged research into new weapons technology abroad that was forbidden in Germany.

Between 1931 and 1933 Kesselring returned to the artillery with command of his own regiment, but his expertise had not escaped Adolf Hitler's notice and, to his initial chagrin, he was reassigned to the RLM. With the death in 1936 of Walther Wever, Hermann Göring's chief of staff in the new Luftwaffe, Kesselring was promoted to take over this position. Like Walter Koch he decided that if he was to be an airman, he had to understand what it took, and learned to fly. Kesselring also later wrote, 'you cannot make war from a desk', and for the invasion of Poland in 1939 he secured command of Luftflotte 1. This was followed in 1940 by similar command of Luftflotte 2 – which included Student's Luftlandekorps – for the invasion of the west. Success was rewarded with a coveted Field Marshal's baton but, as noted earlier, Kesselring became disillusioned during the Battle of Britain and subsequent Blitz by Göring's lack of interest in developing a proper strategic bombing force.[2] Kesselring was never a Nazi either, and regarded the invasion of Russia as a recipe for disaster even though his Luftflotte 2 virtually destroyed the Soviet air force in the first few weeks of the campaign. When the initial impetus of the offensive ran out of steam and the main efforts of the Luftwaffe were diverted to a pointless new blitz on Moscow, Kesselring must have welcomed his re-appointment as Oberbefehlshaber Süd even though he was never given a free rein and ran into constant obstructionism.

In 1942–43, Italian obduracy and reluctance were like weights pinning Kesselring's arms because he had to defer constantly to Maresciallo Ugo Cavallero and his successor, Generale Vittorio Ambrosio, chiefs of staff to Mussolini's Commando Supremo. Rommel's habits of either ignoring instructions completely or going behind his back to the Führer himself were other persistent irritations. When Rommel was ordered on sick leave in March 1943, leaving Panzerarmee Afrika to its fate in Tunisia, Kesselring heaved a sigh of relief even though he was left with the task of salvaging what he could from the wreckage; this included as many as possible of the Fallschirmjäger whose fighting capabilities Kesselring had come to admire and wanted to preserve.

By June an eventual Allied invasion of Italy was a foregone conclusion and Rommel was recalled to head a new Armeegruppe B skeleton staff in Munich. Hitler did not trust the Italians to continue fighting much longer and wanted to establish a firm barrier in the northern Apennines, south of the Alps. When the Allies did invade Sicily on 10 July, Rommel's forces began moving into position. On the 25th, Mussolini was deposed and Rommel's command became independent of Kesselring's Armeegruppe C, which was now entrusted solely with the defence of Italy south of Rome. The two men were at loggerheads once again, with Hitler being persuaded by Rommel that the south was indefensible.

Generalleutnant Heinrich 'Heinz' Trettner
1907 Born 19 September, Minden (Westphalia)
1925–1932 After entering Reichsheer as Fahnenjunker, various postings to infantry and cavalry schools; promoted to Leutnant (1929)
1932–33 Pilot training followed by secondments to Luft Hansa and the Regia Aeronautica; promoted to Oberleutnant (1933)
1933–35 Seconded to the RLM; transferred from Heer to Luftwaffe (May 1934); IIa at Kitzingen and Magdeburg flying schools; promoted to Hauptmann (1935)
1936–37 IIa to Hugo Sperrle in the Legion 'Kondor'
1937–38 Staffelkapitän in KGr 88; Spanish Cross in Gold (1939)
1938–1940 Ia in 7 Flieger Division (July 1938); promoted to Major (August 1939); Stabschef (October 1939); Ritterkreuz (May 1940)
1941–42 Ia in XI Fliegerkorps; promoted to Oberstleutnant (1941)
1942–43 Stabschef in XI Fliegerkorps
1943 Promoted to Oberst (March); entrusted with creating new 4 Fallschirmjäger Division (October)
1944–45 CO of 4 Fallschirmjäger Division; promoted to Generalmajor (July 1944) then Generalleutnant (April 1945); Eichenlaub (September 1944)
1945–48 POW in Britain
1949–56 Civilian appointments until creation of the new Bundeswehr
1956–64 As Generalmajor in the Bundeswehr, various NATO appointments
1964–66 As Generalleutnant, Generalinspekteur der Bundeswehr
1966 Resigned. Trettner was honoured by high decorations, including the US Legion of Merit, the British Royal Victorian Order, French Legion d'Honneur, Italian Order of Merit and Grand Medal Cross of the Federal Republic of Germany. At the time of writing, 'Heinz' Trettner was still alive, age 96

---

2 He was not alone: Erhard Milch, Göring's deputy, fell foul of the Reichsmarschall over the same issue and was eventually dismissed.

(Comparison with Montgomery and Patton is unavoidable.) Kesselring proved them wrong with a masterful withdrawal from Sicily in August and counter-attacking vigorously at Salerno when the Americans landed on 9 September, timing their assault quite deliberately with the Italian secession they had choreographed. In the interim, Kesselring had already begun construction of an elaborate chain of fortifications behind river lines south of Rome – the Gustav Line, which pivoted on Monte Cassino.

This established the ground rules for the remainder of the Italian campaign, with Kesselring restored as overall commander after Rommel's departure to the English Channel coast in November. At the end of the war Kesselring emerged as one of the very few German generals who could have kept his forces in fighting shape during such a long retreat dragged out over nearly another 18 months up the length of Italy. Both 1 and 4 Fallschirmjäger Divisions, alongside the 'Hermann Göring' Division, were crucial elements in forestalling Allied hopes of a quick breakthrough time and time again. Postwar, Kesselring was condemned to death for a number of massacres of Italian civilians but was eventually exonerated and released, partly through the intervention of Winston Churchill himself. Kesselring always fought hard, but like the Fallschirmjäger he commanded, he fought fairly and SS and SD personnel, who were not answerable to the Wehrmacht, carried out most of the atrocities.

Control

Under all the circumstances described above, control of the front-line troops in the Mediterranean theatre was obviously sometimes difficult, which is where the paratroops' ingrained self-control made them so formidable. Many Italians lacked motivation because they believed that they were fighting for the wrong side, although hardcore fascists would keep Mussolini's dream of a new Roman Empire alive to the end. German troops sent to bolster the Italian defence – while not always themselves of top quality – were almost as contemptuous of them as allies as the Anglo-American forces became of them as opponents, with a few exceptions who included Il Paracadutisti. A 'something' that is impossible to quantify with any exactitude welded the paras of both nationalities into a force that remained both disciplined and resolute so that if it had to go down, it would do so with colours flying. A major factor in this was that the rank and file not only had their own self-respect but also were treated with respect by all their officers, and were given the fullest briefings possible about their battlefield objectives. This held them firm in defence and prevented either uncontrolled pursuit of enemy forces on the run, or premature withdrawal from their own positions even when they often seemed untenable.

Communications

Although field telephones, the telegraph and other even more basic methods of battlefield communication remained in widespread use, by 1942 German military radio equipment (Funkgerät) was much more common and varied than it had been during the blitzkrieg era, with many different sets tailored to specific purposes. However, quality suffered somewhat. Before the war, German research by the principal electronics firms Telefunken and Lorenz had resulted in significant advances in ceramics and metallurgy, particularly the alloy Elektron, a high-conductivity compound of aluminium, silver, zinc and other elements. Progress was also made in coils and a serious but never fully successful attempt at some form of standardization resulted in a reduction in the bewildering array of thermionic valves. Other developments included light diecast chassis for the sets, and modular construction within the chassis so that whole sections of the radio could be simply unplugged and replaced while the fault in the original was traced. By 1943, though, supplies of many raw materials were running low and the use of Elektron, for example, was restricted to Luftwaffe sets for air-to-air and air-to-ground communications.

Since the Fallschirmjäger now operated almost solely at ground level, so to speak, the most significant development came from miniaturization, particularly in the fragile valves that took up so much space. The result was the backpack radio that could be carried by one man. All were amplitude modulated (AM) transceivers operating in very high frequency (VHF) bands that lacked an over-the-horizon capability, limiting range in effect to line of sight. The most common model issued to infantry was the Feldfu b that

The man who never was

The Abwehr's failings and the superiority of Allied intelligence were highlighted in early 1943 by the bizarre case of 'Major Martin'. Staring defeat in the face in North Africa with Anglo-American forces closing in on Tunisia from east and west, and after the disaster at Stalingrad, the planners at OKW were asking 'what next?' Little did they realize that the question had already been answered after acrimonious debate during the Casablanca Conference on 23 January. Most senior officers in the United States had favoured a massive build-up in the UK for one decisive cross-Channel onslaught, but the British – with more limited resources and the débâcle of Dieppe sour in the memory – preferred a more oblique approach based on the principle of 'divide and conquer'. In addition, Soviet leader Stalin was pressing for a second front and the worrying possibility existed that, if the western Allies did not act promptly, he might negotiate a separate armistice with Germany. The desired invasion of France could not take place for at least a year because of the huge logistic problems, so something had to be done in the interim. Why not, the British planners argued, use the enormous and experienced forces in Africa for an invasion somewhere on the Mediterranean coast of Europe?

There were several choices: a return to Greece, a link-up with Tito's forces in Yugoslavia as a prelude to an invasion of southern Austria, an assault on the French Riviera – or an attack on Italy both to draw German troops away from France and Russia and, hopefully, result in the collapse of Mussolini's regime. After long discussion, Italy was selected as the target. However, a straightforward invasion of the mainland would have been an unacceptable risk with strong Italian and German air and ground forces remaining on Sicily. The island thus became the first target and the operation was given the codename Husky. In fact, it nearly stopped there, because many Americans in particular felt that capturing the island alone would

pose sufficient threat to tie down substantial German reserves while, as a bonus, Malta would at last be secure.

This was where the British XX ('double cross') Committee came into its own and devised one of the most successful deception plans of the entire war. The inspiration, ironically, came from the Fallschirmjäger. In January 1940 a Messerschmitt Bf 108 liaison aircraft carrying as passenger Hauptmann Helmuth Reinberger – Bassenge's successor as Kommandeur of the Stendal Fliegerschule – had strayed off course and force-landed in Belgium when it ran out of fuel. Reinberger tried to destroy the papers in his briefcase that contained operational details for Luftflotte 2, but neither he nor his pilot were smokers and did not even have a box of matches between them! Although the Allies suspected an attempt at deception, Reinberger's capture caused recriminations in the OKW and a revision of the plans for Fall Gelb.

Remembering all this in the wake of Casablanca, RAF Squadron Leader Sir Archibald Cholmondley from the XX Committee suggested a ruse to draw Axis attention away from Sicily. His people would plant a body carrying convincing papers that would divert the Abwehr's interest elsewhere. And it had to be a corpse so that it could not be interrogated by the Gestapo. Details of the mission were put in the hands of Lieutenant-Commander Ewen Montagu of Naval Intelligence. He had four basic tasks: first, to find a suitable body; second, to decide how to get it into German hands; third, to build a credible false identity for it; and fourth, to create authentic-looking documents. Most of the fascinating story is told in Montagu's book *The Man Who Never Was* and the film of the same title, apart from any mention of 'Ultra' or the real identity of the body that was kept secret for many years in order to save his family embarrassment. His name has latterly emerged as that of a down-and-out Welsh alcoholic, Glyndwr Michael, who died of pneumonia during the winter. The cause of death put fluid in his lungs

consonant with having drowned, so it was decided to land the body ashore from a submarine. Washed up on a beach, it would look as though it had come from a torpedoed ship or ditched aircraft. Then came the delicate task of establishing an identity, painstakingly created as Major William Martin, a fictitious staff officer in the Royal Marines. If he had carried detailed operational plans, they would have fallen under the same suspicion as Reinberger's so, with the connivance of Lord Louis Mountbatten and other senior officers, the briefcase chained to the body's wrist carried personal letters addressed to their counterparts in North Africa. These just gave clues, a reference to sardines being rationed clearly indicating an attack on Sardinia as a possible prelude to an invasion of southern France, and another hinting at the Greek Peloponnese. (Both had been discussed at Casablanca, adding verisimilitude if there had been a 'leak'.) There was a great deal of subtlety and an element of black humour in concocting the letters, and a notice about 'Major Martin' was even put in *The Times* along with the names of genuine officers posted missing. The whole operation was codenamed Mincemeat.

The refrigerated body was duly dropped off the neutral Spanish coast by the Royal Navy submarine *Seraph* on 30 April but the deception did not end there. The British government demanded the return of the briefcase – their insistence underlining its importance. They eventually got it back after its contents had been photocopied for the Abwehr, and 'Major Martin' was buried with full military honours at Huelva in Spain. German intelligence was totally duped and Hitler diverted troops to both Sardinia and Greece; in fact, so seriously did he take the Greek threat that at one point Rommel was briefly made Oberbefehlshaber Südost. Other troops in mainland Italy were also redeployed. These alterations were detected through 'Ultra' and Montagu telegrammed Churchill with the message, 'Mincemeat swallowed whole'.

operated on 90–110Mhz; the same frequency band was employed by Pioniere (Feldfu b1) and Panzergrenadiere (Feldfu b2). With growing war shortages, the ersatz Feldfu c operating on 130–160Mhz became increasingly common. For communicating with their Sturmgeschütze, the Fallschirmjäger used the 23.1–25Mhz Feldfu h, while artillery observers had the 32–38Mhz K1 Fuspr d. All were very heavy by modern standards, but they did greatly improve communications, often down to platoon level, facilitating rapid responses in fluid combat situations that would have been impossible in 1939–41. Strangely, a hand-held frequency modulated (FM) 'walkie-talkie' with a 290km radius and a six-hour battery life, devised by Siemens-Halske in 1942 specifically for the invasion of Malta, was never taken into service.

Intelligence

German intelligence throughout the Mediterranean campaigns was poor, both before and especially after the Italian 'defection'. Hitler tended to regard the whole theatre as a sideshow, so resources were allocated grudgingly and Rommel often had to operate in a virtual intelligence vacuum. The situation was not helped by the multiplicity of agencies that generally refused to cooperate with each other and often mounted simultaneous operations with the same objective, leading to open bureaucratic and sometimes physical conflict. The army, navy and air force each had their own intelligence departments but their efforts were supposedly coordinated by the OKW's central intelligence agency, the Abwehr, headed by Admiral Wilhelm Canaris until his arrest and execution in the wake of the July 1944 attempt on Hitler's life. Thereafter, Ernst Kaltenbrunner's SS-Reichssicherheitshauptamt (RSHA), which had been created under Reinhard Heydrich in 1939 to control the Sicherheitsdienst (SD) and Sicherheitspolizei (Sipo), became responsible for all intelligence and counter-intelligence.

A singular example of the rivalry between the Wehrmacht and SS organizations is the search for Mussolini after King Victor Emmanuel dismissed him on 25 July 1943 and had him spirited away under armed guard. Hitler put all the intelligence assets in Italy into the search for his ally, who was first taken to the small island of Ponza, then to La Maddalena off the Sardinian coast and finally to the Albergo-Rifugio hotel high in the Gran Sasso d'Italia mountains some 130km north-east of Rome. The Abwehr traced him as far as Ponza but then lost him, believing incorrectly that he had been transferred to Elba – where Napoleon had been exiled in 1814. A paratroop rescue was planned using men from III/FJR 7 but abandoned when the SS confirmed he was on La Maddalena instead. He then disappeared again and it was only SS radio intercepts that eventually located him. The paras did drop on Elba anyway, five days after Mussolini's rescue on 12 September, but only to disarm the small Italian garrison because Canaris believed the Allies might want to use the island as a stepping-stone for an amphibious assault behind the Gustav Line. As in the case of Sardinia, they had no intention of island hopping so the Abwehr was hoodwinked once more and the landing at Anzio in January 1944 came as a complete surprise.

Unit organization (1):

7 Flieger Division, 1 June 1941–30 April 1943

When 7 Flieger Division began returning from Crete in June 1941 it was in tatters, having suffered 3,352 fatalities out of an airlanded force of 8,060. It would take time to rebuild even if the OKW permitted it, which was in some doubt for a while. Many senior officers believed that now the element of surprise was forfeit, the enemy would be even more alert to the possibilities of airborne invasion and any future operations would be doomed to costly failure. They had lost sight of the fact that surprise can be achieved through many more means than one. With Göring's backing, Student's forceful persuasion carried the day and he personally supervised the division's gradual reconstruction, even though it would never again fight as a whole.

Alfred Sturm, who had led the division during the ten days of the battle for Crete after Wilhelm Süßmann's death, retained his acting promotion to Generalmajor but reverted to command of FJR 2 from 21 June. Many veterans regarded the choice of new divisional CO as equally odd as that of Süßmann in the first place: Generalleutnant Erich Petersen. A regular army officer, he had commanded the autonomous Infanterie Regiment Nr.125[3] on the relatively quiet Saarbrücken front in May–June 1940 before transferring to the Luftwaffe in October. Despite his lack of paratroop experience, Petersen did have assistance not just from Student himself but also from Süßmann's former chief of staff, Major Conrad-Bernhard Graf von Üxküll. This collaboration lasted until 1 August 1942 when Richard Heidrich assumed command of the division and Petersen moved on, ultimately to lead IV Luftwaffen-Feld Korps (later renamed XL Armeekorps) in France in 1944. Karl-Lothar Schulz then stood in briefly as 7 Flieger Division's chief of staff until Heidrich appointed Major Adolf Haering on 28 August 1942.

Petersen officially assumed command of 7 Flieger Division on 1 June 1941 even though Sturm remained in day-to-day charge on Crete for another three weeks. Most of the men were billeted in British tents, eating tins of 'M&V' that they loathed and Australian peaches that they loved. Australian bush hats were also prized trophies! Gradually between then and early in August the paras were filtered back to their various depots in Germany while replacement platoon, company and battalion leaders were chosen, and the fresh-faced new recruits began to learn lessons from the veterans not taught in the training manuals. By 24 September, though, when the division received mobilization orders for the Ostfront, reconstruction was still far from complete (Fig. 1, page 20, and Table 1,

(continued on page 23)

A bearded paratrooper in the desert. He wears the sand-coloured Luftwaffe tropical tunic, a splinter-camouflaged helmet cover and a blue-grey rifle bandolier; sun-and-sand goggles are slung round his neck.

---

3 By another of those strange coincidences that permeate the Fallschirmjäger story, IR 125 became part of 164 Infanterie Lehr Division – later famous as 164 leichte 'Afrika' Division – when it assumed fortress duty on Crete in January 1942 before being replaced by 22 Luftlande Division (Tropisch) at the end of July.

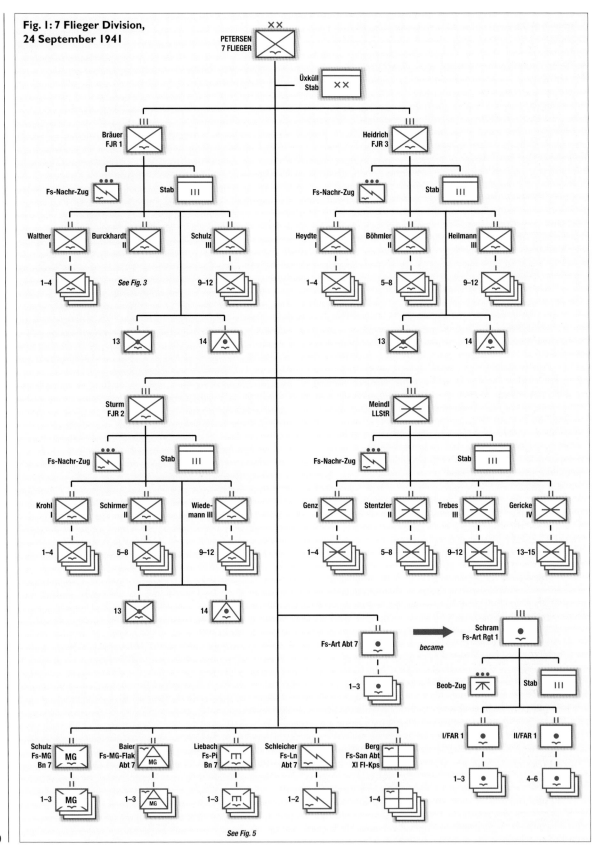

Fig. I: 7 Flieger Division, 24 September 1941

Table 1: 7 Flieger Division, 24 September 1941

Generalleutnant Erich Petersen

Stabschef Major Conrad-Bernhard Graf von Üxküll

Fallschirmjäger Regiment 1 (FJR 1)

Generalmajor Bruno Bräuer

Stabskompanie

I/FJR 1 (*Major Erich Walther*)

    1–3 Jäger-Kompanien

    4 Fallschirm-MG-Kompanie

II/FJR 1 (*Hauptmann Burckhardt*) – becomes Fallschirm-Lehr Bataillon, XI Fliegerkorps

    5–7 Jäger-Kompanien

    8 Fallschirm-MG-Kompanie

III/FJR 1 (*Major Karl-Lothar Schulz*)

    9–11 Jäger-Kompanien

    12 Fallschirm-MG-Kompanie

13 Infanteriegeschütz-Kompanie

14 Panzerjäger-Kompanie

Fallschirmjäger Regiment 2 (FJR 2)

Generalmajor Alfred Sturm

Stabskompanie

I/FJR 2 (*Hauptmann Hans Kroh*)

    1–3 Jäger-Kompanien

    4 Fallschirm-MG-Kompanie

II/FJR 2 (*Hauptmann Gerhard Schirmer*)

    5–7 Jäger-Kompanien

    8 Fallschirm-MG-Kompanie

III/FJR 2 (*Hauptmann Wiedemann*) – becomes III/FJR 4

    9–11 Jäger-Kompanien

    12 Fallschirm-MG-Kompanie

13 Infanteriegeschütz-Kompanie

14 Panzerjäger-Kompanie

Fallschirmjäger Regiment 3 (FJR 3)

Oberst Richard Heidrich

Stabskompanie

I/FJR 3 (*Major Friedrich Freiherr von der Heydte*)

    1–3 Jäger-Kompanien

    4 Fallschirm-MG-Kompanie

II/FJR 3 (*Oberleutnant Rudolf Böhmler*)

    5–7 Jäger-Kompanien

    8 Fallschirm-MG-Kompanie

(continued on page 22)

III/FJR 3 (*Major Ludwig Heilmann*)

    9–11 Jäger-Kompanien

    12 Fallschirm-MG-Kompanie

13 Infanteriegeschütz-Kompanie

14 Panzerjäger-Kompanie

Luftlande-Sturm Regiment (LLStR)

Generalmajor Eugen Meindl (Major Braun acting while Meindl in Russia)

Stabskompanie

I/LLStR (*Oberleutnant Alfred Genz pp. Koch*)

    1–4 Kompanien

II/LLStR (*Major Edgar Stentzler*) – becomes II/FJR 5

    5–8 Kompanien

III/LLStR (*Oberleutnant Horst Trebes*) – becomes III/FJR 5

    9–12 Kompanien

IV/LLStR (*Hauptmann Walther Gericke*)

    13–16 Kompanien

Fallschirm-Artillerie Abteilung 7 reconstructed over winter 1941–42 as:
Fallschirm-Artillerie Regiment 1 (FAR 1)

Hauptmann Bruno Schram

Stabskompanie

    Beobachtungs-Zug

I/FAR 1

    1–3 Batterien

II/FAR 1

    4–6 Batterien

Fallschirm-Luftnachrichten Abteilung 7 (*Major Schleicher*)

    1 & 2 Kompanien

Fallschirm-MG Bataillon 7 (*Major Erich Schulz*)

    1–3 Kompanien

Fallschirm-MG-Flak Abteilung 7 (*Major Hans Baier*)

    1–3 Kompanien

Fallschirm-Pionier Bataillon 1 (*Major Egon Liebach*) reconstructed spring 1942 as:
Fallschirmkorps-Pionier Bataillon (*Major Rudolf Witzig*)

    see text and Fig. 5 (page 30)

Fallschirm-Sanitäts Abteilung XI Fliegerkorps (*Oberfeldarzt Dr von Berg*)

    1–4 Kompanien

The status of the remainder of the division's other sub-units at this time is conjectural so none have been included.

page 21). The Luftlande-Sturm Regiment was never reconstituted as such even though it existed on paper until 26 February 1942. Its CO throughout remained Eugen Meindl although Bernhard Ramcke temporarily assumed the mantle from 21 May to 18 June 1941 when Meindl was wounded, and Major Braun acted as garrison caretaker when he was posted to Russia. In between and afterwards, its four battalions fought independently and soon assumed fresh identities. Other elements of 7 Flieger Division also changed name, such as the artillery, engineer and medical battalions, some becoming corps instead of divisional troops.

Fallschirmjäger deployments to Russia are beyond the scope of this volume so the following is just a brief résumé in order to keep other developments in context. The first units to entrain for the river Neva sector of the Leningrad front were I/ and III/FJR ,1, II/LLStR and 2./Fallschirm-MG Bataillon 7; II/FJR 1 remained behind to become the Korps' Fallschirm-Lehr Bataillon (Fig. 3, page 28). On 1 October II/ and III/FJR 3 arrived and in the middle of the month Petersen, Üxküll and the divisional headquarters also moved east with I/FJR 3 plus 1./Fallschirm-Sanitäts Abteilung and 1., 3. and 4./Fallschirm-Pionier Bataillon 1. The Pioniere in particular suffered such heavy casualties – 1./ was reduced to 37 NCOs and ORs, 3./ from 143 men to 24 and 4./ to just one NCO and ten ORs – that they began withdrawing as early as 16 November to rejoin 2./ which had remained at Dessau as the cadre for the new Fallschirmkorps-Pionier Bataillon (Fig. 5, page 30). The division's total losses soon amounted to approximately 1,000 dead or missing and 2,000 wounded, so the balance of the other units were also returned to Germany and France to recuperate at the beginning of December. Von der Heydte's I/FJR 3 was then chosen to become a second Lehr Bataillon at Döberitz, but this transformation was never completed.

Earlier, FJR 2 along with various sub-units had remained in barracks, but by the end of October a new crisis had arizen, this time in the Ukraine. In November I/ and II/ were reinforced by IV/LLStR, 2./Fallschirm-MG Bataillon 7, 2./Fallschirm-Panzerjäger Abteilung 7 and 2./Fallschirm-Sanitäts Abteilung (replaced by 3./ on 12 December), and formed into a battlegroup under Alfred Sturm. (III/ FJR 2 had already been nominated III/FJR 4 as part of Erich Walther's new regiment in September.) Kampfgruppe 'Sturm' was thrown into action on the river Mius east of Stalino and held the line through January 1942. Over the same period, a second battlegroup under Eugen Meindl had been embroiled to the north, east of Smolensk, principal units being I/LLStR with Walter Koch returned to duty, the regimental headquarters and 1. and 3./Fallschirm-Artillerie Abteilung 7. In February, Meindl's group was sent south to help Sturm's, but not

Fallschirmjäger motorcyclists of a reconnaissance unit in Tunisia, winter 1942/43.

Major Walter Koch, seen in this rather battered snapshot with his head bandaged after being wounded in Tunisia.

for long. A month later a fresh crisis despatched both groups back to the river Volkhov south of Leningrad, close to where the rest of 7 Flieger Division had fought the previous year. Kampfgruppe 'Sturm' was then subordinated to Generalleutnant Wilhelm Bohnstedt's 21 Infanterie Division and incurred such heavy losses in May that not only did Sturm fly to Berlin personally to complain but at the end of June the battlegroup was sent west to France to recuperate, following Koch's I/LLStR from Kampfgruppe 'Meindl'. (Koch's casualties were a staggering 714 men out of an initial complement of 880.) Meindl himself stayed behind with the assault regiment's staff to command a shortlived Luftwaffen Division 'Meindl' comprising Luftwaffen-Feld Regimenter 1–5, a signals battalion and the attached I Luftwaffen-Ski Bataillon.

Although this was not the end of the paras' involvement in the Russian campaign because they were to return after Richard Heidrich became 7 Flieger Division's CO in August, other developments more germane to this narrative demand attention. Since Crete the previous year, Bernhard Ramcke had reverted to officer-in-charge of XI Fliegerkorps' operational training schools, but when provisional plans began taking shape for the invasion of Malta, on 1 March 1942 (Fig. 1a, page 25, and Table 2, below) he was seconded to the Regio Esercito for a month to supervise field instruction for 1° Divisione Paracadutisti 'Folgore' (Fig. 12, page 56). However, it was obvious that, just as in Africa, the Italians would benefit from a physical German presence as well as advisors if the operation were to succeed. Kesselring and Student then had the problem of where to find the men, with Kampfgruppen 'Sturm' and 'Meindl' still embroiled in the east. Fortunately, in February the OKW had already approved the formation of FJR 4 and 5, with III/FJR 2 already allocated to the former. However, FJR 5 was first to began taking shape in May under Oberst Walter Koch – who had actually been nominated for the task on 11 March while still in Russia, such was the

Table 2: 7 Flieger Division composition and strength, October 1942

(numbers in parentheses represent the actual number of parachutists as opposed to the number specified in the TO&E)

	Stab	Transportst.	Schützen-Kp. z.b.V.	FJR 1	FJR 3	FJR 4 *	I/Sturm Rgt.
Officers	26 (25)	3	2 (1)	86 (86)	98 (89)	67 (66)	20 (20)
NCOs	103 (77)	50	28 (3)	885 (812)	698 (595)	551 (472)	218 (209)
Soldiers	201 (97)	38	172 (1)	2,698 (2,255)	2,610 (1,962)	2,118 (1,698)	711 (692)
Total	330 (199)	91	202 (5)	3,669 (3,153)	3,406 (2,646)	2,736 (2,236)	949 (921)

* Only two battalions

Totals:

Officers	511	(421)
NCOs	3,902	(3,051)
Soldiers	15,515	(10,195)
I Fs-Div	19,928	13,667

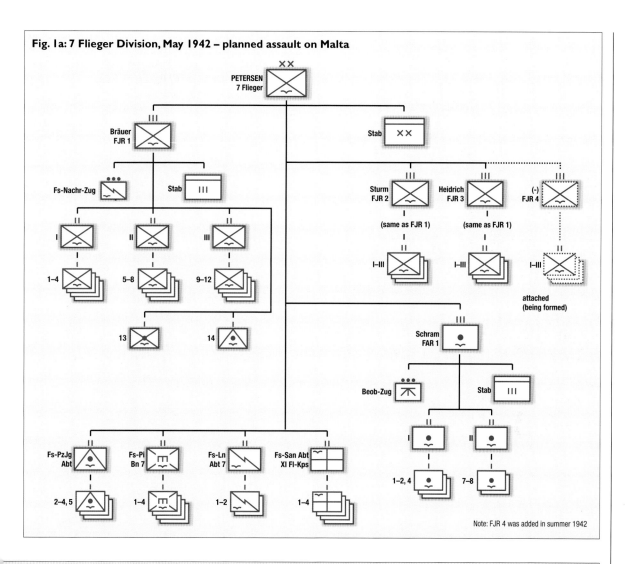

Fig. 1a: 7 Flieger Division, May 1942 – planned assault on Malta

Note: FJR 4 was added in summer 1942

| | | | | | I/Fs-Flak | | | |
I/FAR 1	II/FAR 1	Fs-Pion.Btl	Fs-Pz.Jäg.Abt	Fs-MG Batl.	MG Abt	Fs-Ln.Abt.	San.-Abt.	Services
28 (28)	18	23 (16)	21 (20)	23 (22)	5 (5)	14 (11)	34 (22)	43 (10)
153 (142)	142	158 (141)	198 (167)	169 (146)	44 (44)	88 (58)	144 (120)	273 (65)
627 (441)	500	902 (629)	823 (648)	997 (727)	167 (157)	571 (236)	541 (504)	1,839 (148)
808 (611)	660	1,083 (786)	1,042 (835)	1,189 (895)	216 (206)	673 (305)	719 (646)	2,155 (223)

confusion prevalent within the Fallschirmtruppe during this transitional period. The staff company and Hauptmann Hans Jungwirth's I Bataillon were assembled from scratch; II/FJR 5 was the former II/LLStR now commanded by Major Friedrich Hübner because Edgar Stentzler had been killed in Russia; and III Bataillon was III/LLStR, now commanded by Hauptmann Knoche.

Of these, only Hübner's II/FJR 5 was actually allocated to the invasion force for Malta, along with the equally brand new 1 Fallschirmjäger Brigade under Ramcke authorized on 1 April (Fig. 2, below, and Table 3, page 27). The other elements were initially just Hans Kroh's I/FJR 2 and I/FJR 3 (Lehr), the latter often referred to simply as Bataillon 'von der Heydte'. However, when Operation Herkules was cancelled at the beginning of July, the brigade was enlarged and diverted to North Africa instead. Ramcke himself flew out to Tobruk on the 15th when, even without any men, his command officially became part of Panzerarmee Afrika as the Luftwaffenjäger Brigade. Only a fortnight later, of course, on 1 August Richard Heidrich replaced Petersen as commander of 7 Flieger Division and Oberst Ludwig Heilmann moved up as Chef of FJR 3, with Oberst Erich Walther being chosen to lead the second of the new regiments, FJR 4, that would begin now forming on 1 September. Despite the revitalized, veteran leadership, the process of reconstruction was made virtually impossible by the dispersal of so many units from the south of France to North Africa and Russia.

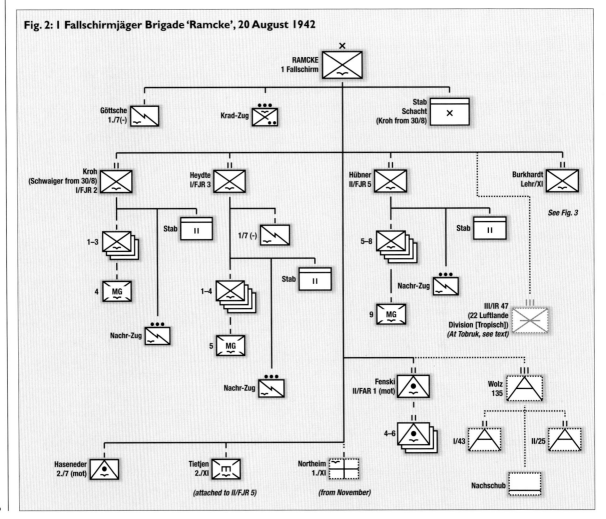

Fig. 2: 1 Fallschirmjäger Brigade 'Ramcke', 20 August 1942

On 4 August, Kroh's I/FJR 2 was staged via Greece to air-land at Tobruk, followed by von der Heydte's expanded I/FJR 3 on the 10th and Hübner's II/FJR 5 on the 17th. They were further reinforced on the 20th by Burkhardt's Fallschirm-Lehr Bataillon XI Fliegerkorps (Fig. 3, page 28), the former II/FJR 1. This unit had actually been in Africa for some months already, operating under 90 leichte Afrika

Table 3: I Fallschirmjäger Brigade 'Ramcke', 20 August 1942

Generalmajor Bernhard Ramcke

Stabschef Hauptmann Gerhard Schacht; from 30 August Major Hans Kroh

I Bataillon (ex-I/FJR 2) *(Major Hans Kroh; from 30 August Hauptmann Schwaiger)*

    1–3 Jäger-Kompanien

    4 Fallschirm-MG-Kompanie

II Bataillon (ex-I/FJR 3) *(Major Friedrich Freiherr von der Heydte)*

    1–4 Jäger-Kompanien

    5 Fallschirm-MG-Kompanie

    1.(Funk)/Fallschirm-Luftnachrichten Abteilung 7(-)*

III Bataillon (ex-II/FJR 5) *(Major Friedrich Hübner)*

    5–8 Jäger-Kompanien

    9 Fallschirm-MG-Kompanie

Fallschirm-Lehr Bataillon (ex-II/FJR 1) *(Hauptmann Burkhardt)*

    1–3 Jäger-Kompanien

    4 Fallschirm-MG-Kompanie

    Artillerie Batterie

    Panzerjäger Batterie**

    Pionier-Sturm Zug

II/Fallschirm-Artillerie Regiment 1 *(Major Fenski)*

    4–6 Batterien (each 4 x 7.5cm GebG36)

1.(Funk)/Fallschirm-Luftnachrichten Abteilung 7(-)** *(Oberleutnant Göttsche)*

2./Fallschirm-Panzerjäger Abteilung 7** *(Oberleutnant Haseneder)*

2./Fallschirmkorps-Pionier Bataillon *(Oberleutnant Cord Tietjen)*

1./Fallschirm-Sanitäts Abteilung [from 15 November] *(Stabsarzt Dr von Northeim)*

135 Flak Regiment [attached] *(Oberst Alwin Wolz)*

    I/43 Flak Abteilung

    II/25 Flak Abteilung

    135 Nachschub-Kolonne

*   *8-man section only.*

** *It is known that the Ramcke Brigade had some 4.2cm PJK 41 tapered-bore guns to complement their old 3.7cm PaK 35/36s, but not how many or in which batteries.*

*** *One platoon only.*

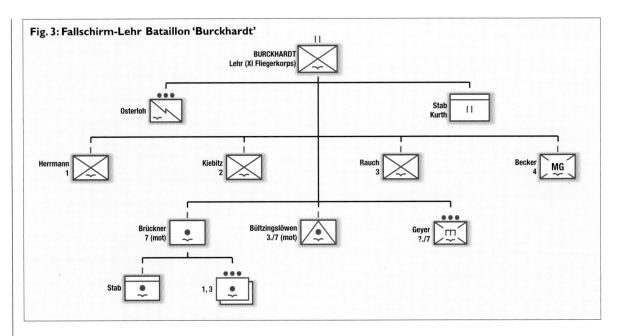

Fig. 3: Fallschirm-Lehr Bataillon 'Burckhardt'

Division. (It should be noted that a Lehr or 'demonstration' unit in the Wehrmacht was not, as the name implies, merely a showpiece formation but had a much more serious function as a test and evaluation cadre for new equipment and tactical ideas. The battalion therefore had additional artillery and anti-tank batteries, plus an assault engineer platoon.) Von der Heydte's battalion (Fig. 2) was also of unusual composition.

The Ramcke Brigade, as it quickly became colloquially known, incorporated organic signals, artillery, anti-tank and engineer companies but had no anti-aircraft defence or supply train until Rommel added 135 Flak Regiment from 19 Flak Division to its strength, also on 20 August. There were no medical services until November, and no MT section. Estimates of the brigade's strength vary. Ramcke's own verbal report to Rommel on 16 July said 2,000 effectives plus the artillery and anti-tank companies, but this does not appear to include Burckhardt's battalion. The Flak and other attachments obviously raised the figure even further so that, according to Pz.AOK Afrika records, on the eve of Alamein it was 4,610 – far stronger than a British brigade, but much weaker than the Scottish 50th Tyne/Tees Division on the other side of the minefields. However, this was only the beginning of Fallschirmjäger deployments to North Africa (Fig. 4, page 29).

After a plan to use the Ramcke Brigade to capture selected bridges over the river Nile in September was sensibly scrapped, the paras were instead allocated positions slightly right of centre in the Alamein line with the 'Folgore' Division further to their south. The new idea was that they would be used as ground reinforcements to exploit Rommel's hoped-for breakthrough towards Cairo and Suez. Quite how they would have accomplished this without adequate motor transport is unclear. Montgomery's Operation Lightfoot launched on 23 October thwarted this plan anyway, and on 2 November Ramcke was ordered to withdraw his brigade 30km west in a night march. Within two days this was insufficient and he was ordered a further 150km back to Fuka. By this time the British had virtually cut off his line of retreat, so such a trek on foot across the inhospitable desert must have seemed impossible. Regardless, Ramcke rallied what he could of his scattered command, broke out of the encirclement (losing 450 men in the process) and set off north-west to intersect the coast road. Rommel had already written the brigade off as lost, but on 6 November the remaining 600-plus paras rolled in

Fig. 4: XI Fliegerkorps deployments to North Africa, August 1942–May 1943

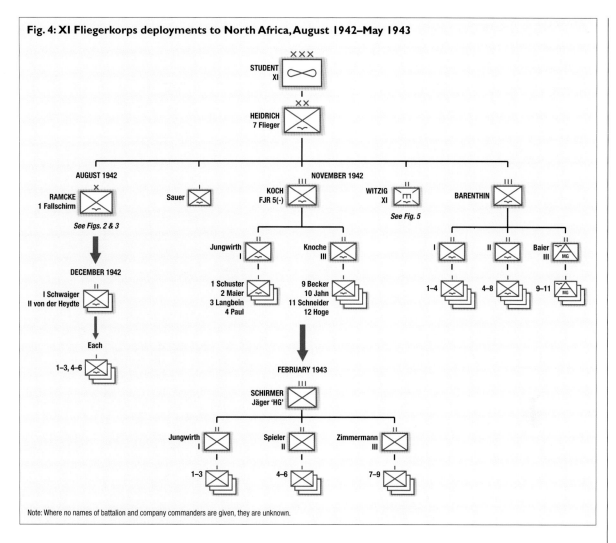

Note: Where no names of battalion and company commanders are given, they are unknown.

style into the new German lines, having ambushed a British convoy complete with plentiful supplies of whisky and cigarettes! As further stragglers came in, Ramcke and Kroh subsequently reorganized them into two weak composite battalions under von der Heydte and Major Schwaiger, each with just three companies. By then, however, they had reverted to just being the Luftwaffenjäger Brigade because Ramcke himself was flown back to Germany and played no further role in North Africa, being promoted to Generalleutnant on 21 December 1942 and entrusted with command of the new 2 Fallschirmjäger Division on 13 February 1943 (see next chapter).

Any sense of jubilation at Ramcke's escape from Alamein evaporated on 8 November when news began arriving of the Anglo-American amphibious landings in Morocco and Algeria (Operation Torch). It was clear that the Allies' first objective would be an eastward sweep into Tunisia in order to trap Panzerarmee Afrika between Montgomery's hammer and the new anvil. At this point Hitler decided belatedly to permit Rommel some of the reinforcements that had been so long denied. To begin with, though, there was precious little for Kesselring to send, but the Fallschirmjäger were first off the mark (Fig. 4, above).

The most readily available units were the two remaining battalions (1.–4.I/ and 9.–12./III/) of Koch's FJR 5 at Reims. However, only three weeks earlier, on 15 October, these had been assigned to the 'General Göring' Brigade as part of

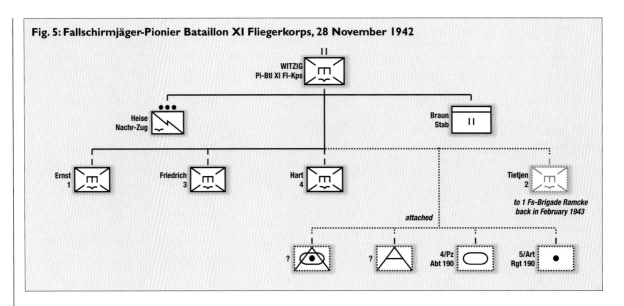

Fig. 5: Fallschirmjäger-Pionier Bataillon XI Fliegerkorps, 28 November 1942

WITZIG
Pi-Btl XI Fl-Kps

Heise
Nachr-Zug

Braun
Stab

Ernst
1

Friedrich
3

Hart
4

Tietjen
2

*to 1 Fs-Brigade Ramcke
back in February 1943*

attached

? | ? | 4/Pz Abt 190 | 5/Art Rgt 190

its expansion into the 'General Göring' Division. This created a clerical nightmare because the regiment temporarily appeared on the TO&E of both XI Fliegerkorps and the new formation. Moreover, a number of men from FJR 5 and the Fallschirmkorps-Pionier Bataillon had already begun assembling in Athens prior to their anticipated move to join the Ramcke Brigade. Uncaring of which parent organization they now belonged to, Kesselring collected them, together with other paras convalescing from sickness or injury, into a composite company that was inserted into Tunis on 8 November even while the Allies were still streaming ashore to their west. Command of the tiny force was entrusted to Hauptmann Sauer, who was tasked with organizing the defence of Tunis's El Aouina and La Marsa airports. This first Fallschirmjäger contingent was closely followed over 12–16 November as described earlier by Stab and I/ and III/FJR 5; and on the 15th by Dr Northeim's 1./Fallschirm-Sanitäts Bataillon plus the balance of Witzig's 716-strong Pionier Bataillon (Fig. 5, above). Both were very welcome but the Pioniere for the unusual reason that the battalion included a signals platoon; up to this point the newly arrived paras had no radios so runners had to rely on the Tunis tram network!

For the most part, the Fallschirmjäger were deployed semi-independently in small task forces to seize high ground and river crossings to the west of Tunis pending the arrival of conventional infantry, and armour. They were joined later in November by the unnumbered Luftwaffen-Regiment 'Barenthin', a hastily created ad hoc formation of two so-called parachute battalions (1–4./I and 5–8./II) plus the three 20mm batteries of Oberst Hans Baier's former Fallschirm-MG-Flak Abteilung 7, redesignated 9–11./III. Overall strength is unknown, but the infantry did include a high proportion of Pioniere because Generalmajor Walter Barenthin, an army engineer who had transferred to the Luftwaffe as XI Fliegerkorps' senior Pionier officer, commanded the regiment. After he was wounded on 10 March 1943, Baier took over the regiment up to the final surrender on 13 May.

Meanwhile, on 19 February FJR 5 was officially redesignated Jäger-Regiment 'Hermann Göring' as part of a Kampfgruppe from the 'General Göring' Division under Oberst Josef Schmid that had begun arriving in Tunisia in December. II/FJR 5, which had fought as part of the Ramcke Brigade, had been disbanded after Alamein, so I/ and III/ alone were reorganized into the understrength I–III/Jäger-Bataillone 'HG', each now of just three companies. Koch was invalided back to Germany at the same time so the renamed regiment was commanded by Major Gerhard Schirmer until 20 April when he

The Germans allowed proxy marriages for soldiers serving abroad and here, in the Western Desert, Oberst Bernhard Ramcke looks on paternally as a member of his brigade signs the documents marrying him to a girl back home.

(and Hans Jungwirth) were repatriated; the regiment's final Chef when it surrendered on 13 May was Hauptmann Zimmermann.

By this juncture 7 Flieger Division itself had passed into history, dissolved on 30 April but resurrected the following day as 1 Fallschirmjäger Division. One footnote remains: the division's very last parachute drop. On the afternoon of 29 December 1942 a dozen Ju 52s took off from Bizerta airfield, six of them towing DFS 230s, with Oberleutnant Friedrich's 3./Fallschirm-Pionier Bataillon aboard. Their objectives were airfields and bridges behind Allied lines in the Tebessa area, with the idea of sabotaging communications and supplies. It was a poorly conceived scheme from the start, compounded by inept navigation and pilot error in the gathering dusk of an overcast and windy day. None of the paras landed anywhere near their targets, there were many injuries from misjudged glider landings, and the Fallschirmjäger were quickly rounded up by British patrols. It made an undignified end to the illustrious history of 7 Flieger Division, but the new 1 and 2 Fallschirmjäger Divisions would quickly show that the traditions created were still very much alive.

Messerschmitt Me 321 and Me 323 – the giants of the sky

On 20 May 1941, KGzbV 1 under Oberst Fritz Morzik was flying Fallschirmjäger to Crete in Ju 52s and DFS 230s. Mission accomplished, Morzik was given a fresh one the same month as CO of (GS)Kdo 1 flying brand new Me 321s. A year later, 12 of these aircraft from (GS)Kdo 2 were to have helped spearhead the airlanding assault on Malta.

The idea of a giant (Gigant) glider capable of carrying a whole company of infantry, a PzKpfw IV tank or alternative loads up to 22 tonnes, emerged from the planning for Operation Sëelowe. The resulting machine had a cavernous 28m fuselage with a clamshell nose and a wingspan of 55m. The only aircraft capable of towing it off the ground on their own, even with RATO, were the Ju 290 – transport derivative of Erhard Milch's abandoned strategic bomber – and the 'Siamese twin' He 111Z. Some 200 Me 321s were built, and they were used for ferrying troops and supplies to Tunisia and Russia, but not for airlanding the Fallschirmjäger.

The same was regrettably true of the Me 323, also christened Gigant. This was a six-engine version of the glider, with troops seated on two decks, but at 43 tonnes fully laden it still needed help getting off the ground, and maximum speed of 218km/h was only 6km/h faster than the glider. Unsurprisingly, both aircraft also needed power-assisted controls, and were so vulnerable to enemy fighters that armament was steadily increased to 12 machine guns and two 20mm cannon.

Me 323s of I/ and II/KGrzbV 323 flying from Trapani in Sicily were used to reinforce Rommel in Tunisia, but the most audacious use would have been that suggested by Kurt Student in 1943 when he called for the formation of a Luftlande-Panzergrenadier division with 126 AFVs and two regiments of paratroops to be carried in 150 Me 321s/323s and 300 DFS 230s/Go 242s. Needless to say, it never materialized.

Unit organization (2):

1 Fallschirmjäger Division, 1 May 1943–2 May 1945; 2 Fallschirmjäger Division, 13 February–17 November 1943; 4 Fallschirmjäger Division, 11 May 1943–4 May 1945

By the time 7 Flieger Division changed its name, elements of 2 Fallschirmjäger Division were already in existence although not yet fully trained nor up to strength. As stated earlier, Bernhard Ramcke was flown home from Africa at the end of November 1942, promoted Generalleutnant on 21 December and appointed commander of the new formation on 13 February 1943. At the time, it was based around Vannes in Brittany, under 7 Armee, but during May moved to the vicinity of Arles and Nîmes in the Rhône valley as part of XI Fliegerkorps, Heeresgruppe D. Surprisingly, Erich Walther's FJR 4, which had begun forming

Soon after the seizure of the Eternal City, a line was drawn at St Peter's Square separating the Vatican from the rest of the city. For a while, Fallschirmjäger undertook security and patrol duties outside the Vatican. (Count E.G. Vitetti collection)

on 1 September 1942, was not involved but was instead allocated to 7 Flieger Division until 1 May 1943 when it became 1 Fallschirmjäger Division's third regiment. Alfred Sturm's FJR 2 was still in Russia, minus III/ that had been redesignated III/FJR 4 in November when the rest of the regiment went east.

On Crete two years previously, 7 Flieger Division had simply consisted of FJR 1–3 plus the semi-autonomous LLStR and artillery, etc. Two years later many changes were in process: firstly, the division was being gathered into a strategic reserve, much like the US 82nd and 101st Airborne in November 1944; secondly, it was being transformed into an infantry division with special talents. At the time of the name change, the bulk of Heidrich's men were stationed at Flers, near Caen in Normandy, but moved south to Avignon later in the month, closer to 2 Fallschirmjäger Division. Both divisions were therefore relatively near to hand when the invasion of Sicily began on 9/10 July 1943, yet Hitler decided that at the moment only one of them was to be transferred to Italy (Fig. 6, below).

On 11 July FJR 3 was airlifted to Rome, the vanguard of 1 Fallschirmjäger Division, preceded by Richard Heidrich and his staff. After a brief conference with Generalfeldmarschall Kesselring at his HQ in Frascati, who gave him the

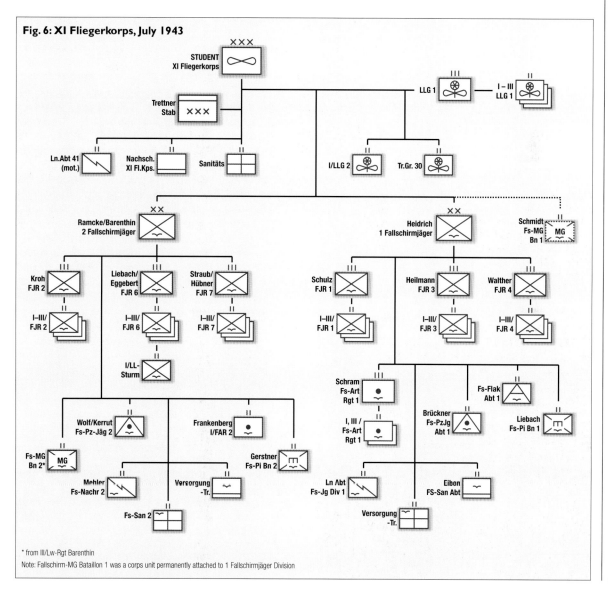

Fig. 6: XI Fliegerkorps, July 1943

* from III/Lw-Rgt Barenthin

Note: Fallschirm-MG Bataillon 1 was a corps unit permanently attached to 1 Fallschirmjäger Division

Strength and weaponry

Divisional war strengths established in 1943 gave every Fallschirmjäger division a total manpower of some 17,000 men, of which about two-thirds made up the 'combat strength'. This consisted of units assigned to front-line duty and excluded divisional services and other rear echelon units. The bulk of the divisional combat strength was in the three Fallschirmjäger regiments, each one having three battalions of three rifle companies and one machine-gun company. Every regiment also had a mortar and an anti-tank company plus, since May 1944, a pioneer company. Regimental war establishment strength was 3,206, while every battalion had an established strength of 853. A rifle company had an established strength of 170 men, and its armament included 20 light machine-guns, three light anti-tank rifles (to be replaced by rocket launchers) and three light 50mm mortars. A machine-gun company was 205 strong and its armament included eight heavy and four medium mortars, plus two light 75mm infantry guns (recoilless). The mortar company was 163 strong, and its armament included 12 heavy 120mm mortars and three light machine guns. The anti-tank company was 186 strong and was equipped with 14 towed 75mm anti-tank guns, plus anti-tank guns or rocket launchers. The pioneer company had about 100 men. The artillery regiment was composed of three battalions each with three batteries, it was 1,571 strong and was equipped with 24 105mm light howitzers (first and second battalion) and 12 150mm heavy howitzers (third battalion). The Panzerjäger battalion had 484 men in three companies, each equipped with 12 towed 75mm guns. Its structure was expanded in 1944 until it was to have six companies, which included self-propelled anti-tank guns. Since late 1943 every division was to acquire a Flak (anti-aircraft) battalion, which was to be 824 strong. It was composed of five batteries, three equipped with six towed 88mm dual purpose guns and two light batteries each equipped either with 12 self-propelled 20mm or 37mm guns.

task of closing a gap in Sicily's frontline along with Kampfgruppe 'Schmalz' of the 'Hermann Göring' Division, Heidrich issued orders to transport the various units of the division to Sicily by air as soon as they arrived in Italy. Promptly, on the afternoon of 12 July Heilmann's 1,400-strong FJR 3 was airdropped on the Catania plains and made contact with Kampfgruppe 'Schmalz', to whom it was subordinated. Incidentally, this was to be the last large-scale German airdrop of World War II. FJR 3 was followed on 13 July by Fallschirm-MG Bataillon 1, which moved south immediately after landing at Catania airport, and by the Funk-Kompanie of Luftnachrichten-Abteilung 1. Other units also arrived at Catania airport; two companies of Fallschirm-Pionier Bataillon 1, the first Abteilung of Fallschirm-Artillerie Regiment 1 and three platoons (1, 5, 6) of Fallschirm-Panzerjäger Abteilung 1.

Soon after their seizure of Rome, Fallschirmjäger of 2 FJD undertook security and control duties in the city. Here a patrol watches over the northern approaches of the bridges over the Tiber; the Castel Sant'Angelo is in the background. (Count E.G. Vitetti collection)

None of them had time to rest, for on the very same day the German situation in Sicily became critical: on 13 July the town of Augusta fell into British hands and, on the night of 13/14 July, British paratroopers and Commandos seized the bridges on the Simeto and Lentini Rivers just south of Catania, thus cutting out both Kampfgruppe 'Schmalz' and FJR 3. The situation was saved by the intervention of Hauptmann Stangenberg, a 1 Fallschirmjäger Division staff officer, who organized an 'alarm unit' using men from both the Funk-Kompanie and a nearby Flak unit and promptly counter-attacked. Soon a Kampfgruppe composed of two companies of Fallschirm-Pionier Bataillon 1 and Fallschirm-MG Bataillon 1 joined them. Until 17 July the area saw savage fighting between the 'Grün Teufel' and the 'Red Devils', but eventually British armour and infantry reached the Simeto. As a result, Kampfgruppe 'Schmalz' and FJR 3 had to move north on the western side of Mt Etna while its eastern side was defended by the newly arrived FJR 4 (minus 8./II, two platoons each from 5 and 7./II and 14./FJR 4), which, together with Fallschirm-MG Bataillon 1, Fallschirm-Pionier Bataillon 1, Fallschirm-Panzerjäger Abteilung 1 and the units from Fallschirm-Artillerie Regiment 1, formed Kampfgruppe 'Walther'.

It took nearly a month before the two groups rejoined south of Messina where, since 10 August, the Germans had begun the evacuation of their troops to the Italian mainland. Until 17 August, when the Allies entered Messina, the defence line was manned by men of the 'Hermann Göring' and 1 Fallschirmjäger Divisions. The losses had been appalling, a common occurrence in the history of the Fallschirmjäger. Of the 1,400 men of FJR 3 no less than 1,100 had been killed, captured or wounded, and the regiment had only had 200 replacements. Fallschirm-MG Bataillon 1 was in no better shape, for in early September its strength was only 150.

Between mid- and late July the rest of 1 Fallschirmjäger Division, mainly its reinforced FJR 1, moved to Naples. Soon after Mussolini's downfall on 25 July, Student's XI Fliegerkorps and Ramcke's 2 Fallschirmjäger Division were rushed to Rome on Hitler's orders, officially to defend the city but actually ready to undertake Operation Schwarz (Black), the intention of which was to free Mussolini and take over the country. When the Italian surrender was announced on the afternoon of 8 September the Germans immediately began Operation Achse (Axis), disarming Italian troops in northern and central Italy and seizing the country. A few hours later, Allied troops landed at Salerno. Once more, the Fallschirmjäger were to play a vital role in these events.

With about 80 per cent of its established strength, some 14,000 men, 2 Fallschirmjäger Division was to face no less than two coastal and four Italian infantry divisions in Rome. The city itself was also defended by two other armoured divisions (one of which, the 'Centauro', was considered unreliable by Italian commanders since it was composed of Mussolini's 'Blackshirts'), plus elements of another infantry division that was being moved from the north. Student's XI Fliegerkorps could only rely on 2 Fallschirmjäger Division, stationed on the coast south of Rome, which was under strength (II/FJR 6 was at Foggia and most of FJR 7 was held in reserve for airborne operations), and on 3 Panzergrenadier Division stationed well north of Rome. A few hours after the announcement of the Italian surrender, 2 Fallschirmjäger Division had disarmed two Italian coastal divisions and seized the coastline near Rome.

A Fallschirmjäger overlooks a crowd of Roman locals, probably immediately after the ceasefire of 10 September. He is carrying a captured Italian Beretta 9mm sub-machine gun, later pressed into German service as the MP38/40. The weapon has a 40-round magazine and an upside-down fixed bayonet. (Count E.G. Vitetti collection)

I Fallschirm-Korps

The first field corps headquarters of the Fallschirmjäger was formed in Italy on 28 December 1943, using personnel from both XI Fliegerkorps and II Luftwaffe-Feld Korps. It was activated on 22 January 1944 and was deployed against the Anzio beachhead containing 4 Fallschirmjäger and 65 Infanterie Divisions, to which 3 Panzergrenadier Division was later added. In June 1944 it withdrew north of Rome and was subsequently deployed in the area around Florence, Futa Pass and Bologna. Until 15 November 1944 it was commanded by General der Fallschirmtruppe Alfred Schlemm

who, after he took over command of the I Fallschirm-Armee from Student, was replaced by Generalleutnant Richard Heidrich, formerly commander of I Fallschirmjäger Division. Corps troops included the Artillerie Kommandeur 122 (Artillery Commander 122, an army unit), the Luft-Nachrichten Abteilung I Fallschirm-Korps (communications), the Fallschirm-Aufklärungs Abteilung 11 (reconnaissance), the Fallschirm-Artillerie Regiment 11 (artillery regiment) and the Fallschirm-Sturmgeschütz Brigade 11. Incidentally, this had been created from the Fallschirm-Sturmgeschütz Brigade 1 der Luftwaffe and was renamed as such in

June 1944. Employed for the first time at Anzio on 22 January 1944, it was mainly equipped with Italian self-propelled anti-tank guns. It was also known as Sturmgeschütz-Abteilung 'Schmidt' after the name of its commander. Other corps troops included the Fallschirm-Flak Regiment 11 and the Fallschirm-Maschinengewehr Bataillon 1, the latter permanently attached to the I Fallschirmjäger Division. Supply was provided by the Führer der Nachschubeinheiten 11. Between January and the final surrender in April 1945, I Fallschirm-Korps consisted of both I and 4 Fallschirmjäger Divisions.

A Feldwebel (note the rank insignia on his right arm) of 2 Fallschirmjäger Division watches a column of Italian soldiers walking away in the centre of Rome. (Count E.G. Vitetti collection)

The following morning II/FJR 6 was airdropped at Monterotondo, east of Rome, in an attempt to capture the Italian Comando Supremo, though they had evacuated their HQ some hours before. During the ensuing fight II/FJR 6 captured no fewer than 2,500 Italian soldiers at the cost of 33 dead and 88 wounded. In the meantime the bulk of 2 Fallschirmjäger Division, commanded by its Ia (first staff officer) von der Heydte,[4] moved to the centre of Rome. There was heavy fighting at the southern gate of the city, but by the morning of 10 September the Fallschirmjäger had reached the city centre. In the afternoon the Italians agreed a ceasefire, which included the disarming of most of their units. With Rome declared an 'open city', most of the Fallschirmjäger came back to defend the coast. The seizure of the Eternal City had cost 109 dead and 510 wounded. Although 2 Fallschirmjäger Division units carried out other airborne operations (Mors' I/FJR 7 spectacular rescue of Mussolini at Gran Sasso; Hübner's III/FJR 7 seizure of the island of Elba; and Kühne's I/FJR 2 airdrop on to the Aegean island of Leros), it was subsequently employed in security duties on the Tyrrhenian coastline.

In the first days of September, 1 Fallschirmjäger Division was split in three groups: I and II/FJR 1 (plus 8./II, two platoons each from 5 and 7./II and 14./FJR 4) along with other divisional units were at Taranto in Apulia; III/FJR 1 was at Naples; and the other divisional units, plus remnants of FJR 3 and 4, were in Calabria, Italy's southern tip. Soon after the British landing at Reggio Calabria on 3 September, many units were sent to Apulia in the Taranto–Bari area; these included Fallschirm-MG Bataillon 1, Fallschirm-Pionier Bataillon 1, Fallschirm-Panzerjäger Abteilung 1 and Fallschirm-Artillerie Regiment 1. After the Italian surrender, the landing at Salerno and the British airborne landing at Taranto on 9 September, every unit of 1 Fallschirmjäger Division was committed; III/FJR 1 went to Salerno with the 'Hermann Göring' Division and was soon followed by I/FJR 3, II/FJR 3 and the bulk of FJR 4. In Apulia III/FJR 3 formed part of a Kampfgruppe with the rest of FJR 4 and, along with I/FJR 1 and other divisional units, fought against both the Italians and the British forces.

Eventually the Germans were forced to abandon their counter-attacks at Salerno and, on 19 September, 1 Fallschirmjäger Division was given the task of covering the German withdrawal. On 19/20 September II/FJR 1 and the bulk of FJR 4 rejoined the division, being followed by other units throughout late September and early October. At this stage 1 Fallschirmjäger Division was holding a 70km-wide front with less than a quarter of its established combat strength, about 1,300 men. At the end of September the division withdrew from the area of Foggia and, by 20 October, it took over the defence of the

---

4 Generalleutnant Ramcke was on sick leave; a few days later Generalmajor Barenthin took over command.

Fallschirmjäger of 2 FJD manning a 75mm PaK 40 in Rome, September 1943. This was quite an unusual weapon for such a unit, since Fallschirm-Panzerjäger Abteilungen were mostly equipped with the 50mm PaK 38. (Count E.G. Vitetti collection)

Trigno River line. It subsequently withdrew behind the Sangro River in November, by which time its divisional combat strength had risen to 185 officers and 6,542 other ranks thanks to replacements. By mid-December 1943 the British Eighth Army attacked Ortona and the town was initially defended by II/FJR 3 and attached units. By 19 December the entire division was moved to Ortona where it fought tenaciously until the 28th, when the town fell into British/Canadian hands. After a month of relative lull, on 31 January 1944 the division received the order to move to Cassino.

November 1943 marked a series of reorganizations amongst the Fallschirmjäger. While still in the Rome area 2 Fallschirmjäger Division had been strengthened: in October II/FJR 5 (composed of remnants of FJR 5) was attached, while Fallschirm-MG Bataillon 2 (from III/Luftwaffe-Regiment 'Barenthin', redesignated in early 1944 Fallschirm-Granatenwerfer Bataillon 2), Fallschirm-Flak Bataillon 2 and II/Fallschirm-Artillerie Regiment were formed. In late November the division left Italy for the Eastern Front leaving behind III/FJR 6 (attached to 3 Panzergrenadier Division), I/FJR 7 (which became Fallschirmjäger-Lehr Bataillon) and other units used to create the cadres of the new 4 Fallschirmjäger Division: I/FJR 2 (which became I/FJR 10), II/FJR 6 (became I/FJR 11) and I/Luftlande-Sturm Regiment 1 (became I/FJR 12), which had been attached to FJR 6 during the summer. XI Fliegerkorps also left Italy for France, where it formed the 1 Fallschirm-Armee, leaving behind elements used to create I Fallschirm-Korps on 28 December 1943.

Formed on 5 November 1943 in a vast area north of Rome, 4 Fallschirmjäger Division (Fig. 8, page 41) was the first of a series of new Fallschirmjäger divisions to be created in the final years of the war. Commanded by Oberst Heinrich Trettner, formerly Ia of 7 Flieger Division, the division was built using both new recruits and personnel from other Luftwaffe units gathered around a

According to the ceasefire agreement of 10 September 1943, two Italian battalions of the Piave Division were left in Rome for security duties. In mid-October they were disarmed and disbanded. Here we see Fallschirmjäger conferring with Italian officers whilst Italian soldiers are carried away aboard lorries. The main photograph is interesting as it shows three Fallschirmjäger, each equipped with a different weapon: from left to right, an FG42, an MP40 and the ubiquitous Kar 98 rifle. (Count E.G. Vitetti collection)

This is the first in a series of three photos showing a group of Fallschirmjäger captured in May 1945 at the end of the war by the Royal Italian Army. (Archivio Ufficio Storico Stato Maggiore Esercito (AUSSME) – via Filippo Cappellano)

cadre of experienced and battle-tested Fallschirmjäger. As early as 18 January 1944 it formed an 'Einsatzgruppe' (intervention group), which was moved south of Rome to combat any possible Allied landing in the area. This actually took place on 22 January 1944 at Anzio, and immediately some 1,100 men of Kampfgruppe 'Gericke' (FJR 11) moved against the beachhead. On the same day battalions 'Hauber' (II/FJR 2) and 'Kleye' reached the town of Ardea, supported by two companies of Fallschirm-Pionier Bataillon 4 and Sturmgeschütz-Abteilung 'Schmidt', plus other army units. In the following days the rest of Gericke's FJR 11 reached the beachhead, being put under Kampfgruppe 'Pfeiffer' of 65 Infanterie Division. Between 25 and 27 January, Kampfgruppe 'Schulz' of 1 Fallschirmjäger Division (I, II/FJR 1, III/FJR 3, Fallschirm-MG Bataillon 1) also arrived along with Hermann's Fallschirm-Lehr Bataillon, which had been reforming in Florence. These were put under control of the 'Hermann Göring' Division in the Ardea area (Fig. 7, page 40, along with Table 4, page 29, and Fig. 8, page 41).

In early February, while the rest of 4 Fallschirmjäger Division (FJR 10 and the Sturm FJR 12) reached Anzio, the first clashes occurred. On 30 January III/FJR 11 drove back an American attack at Cisterna, and on 7 February there was a counter-attack in the Carroceto–Aprilia area. Between 16 and 20 February the Germans made the first major counter-attack against the beachhead, which involved five companies from FJR 11 and 12 along with one from Fallschirm-Pionier Bataillon 4 at the Buonriposo Ridge, while during the second German counteroffensive (29 February–2 March) elements of FJR 10 and 11 fought in the 'Caves' area. Losses were heavy, particularly in the Fallschirm-Lehr Bataillon: it was practically destroyed on 16 February 1944 and had to be sent to France for rest and refit. The end of German major offensives did not mean, however, that Anzio became a quiet place, rather the opposite. On 7–8 March FJR 10 repulsed a heavy attack, but it suffered so many losses that it had to be pulled out of the line and put in reserve.

(continued on page 43)

Table 4: I Fallschirmjäger Division, I February 1944

Generalleutnant Richard Heidrich

Stabschef Major G. Heckel

Feldgendarmerie-Zug (mot)

Kradschützen-Zug

Fallschirmjäger Regiment 1 (FJR 1)

Oberst Karl-Lothar Schulz

Stab

Nachrichten-Zug

Kradschützen-Zug

Pionier-Zug

I/FJR 1 (*Major Werner von der Schulenberg*)

   1–3 Jäger-Kompanien

   4 Fallschirm-MG-Kompanie

II/FJR 1 (*Major Gröschke*)

   5–7 Jäger-Kompanien

   8 Fallschirm-MG-Kompanie

III/FJR 1 (*Major Karl-Heinz Becker*)

   9–11 Jäger-Kompanien

   12 Fallschirm-MG-Kompanie

13 Infanteriegeschütz-Kompanie

14 Panzerjäger-Kompanie

Nachschubkolonne (mot)

Fallschirmjäger Regiment 3 (FJR 3)

Oberst Heilmann

Stab

Nachrichten-Zug

Kradschützen-Zug

Pionier-Zug

I/FJR 3 (*Major Böhmler*)

   1–3 Jäger-Kompanien

   4 Fallschirm-MG-Kompanie

II/FJR 3 (*Hauptmann Foltin*)

   5–7 Jäger-Kompanien

   8 Fallschirm-MG-Kompanie

III/FJR 3 (*Major Kratzert*)

   9–11 Jäger-Kompanien

   12 Fallschirm-MG-Kompanie

The 'fire brigades'

Having been created for airborne operations, the use of Fallschirmjäger divisions in land warfare was not particularly apt, especially in defensive roles. Until mid-1944 they lacked heavy weapons, mostly heavy artillery, and the lack of motorization made them not very suitable in their new role. Then there are two questions to answer: how come they got to be employed exactly in that role, and how did they prove to be so successful? The answer to the first question can be found in the tactics of the 'Fuerwehr' (fire brigades), which the Germans successfully developed since 1943. Because of the progressive deterioration of their land units combat values, the Germans focused on a series of elite units which were accorded a priority in the allocation of both weapons and replacements. These got to be used as fire brigades which were to be deployed in endangered sectors of the front, either in a defensive or in an offensive role. This way they were able to make up for the weaknesses of the other average units, which all too often collapsed under a strong enemy attack. Needless to say, mobile units (both Panzer and Panzergrenadier, in particular Waffen-SS) were chosen for this role, although other elite units also included the Fallschirmjäger divisions. The reason for such a choice is simple to explain and leads us to answering the second question too: the most valuable quality of an elite unit is the high spirit and morale of its men. These qualities, along with the precious battle experience acquired by the veterans, were passed on to the new recruits by the units' cadres, generally speaking composed of battle-hardened officers and NCOs. That enabled elite units to face hard tests again and again in spite of their losses, at least until they were provided the needed amount of replacements, weapons, equipment and supplies. Until this system kept working, units like the I Fallschirmjäger Division proved capable of facing one task after another, no matter how hard and difficult they could be.

(continued on page 42)

Fig. 7: I Fallschirmjäger Division, I February 1944

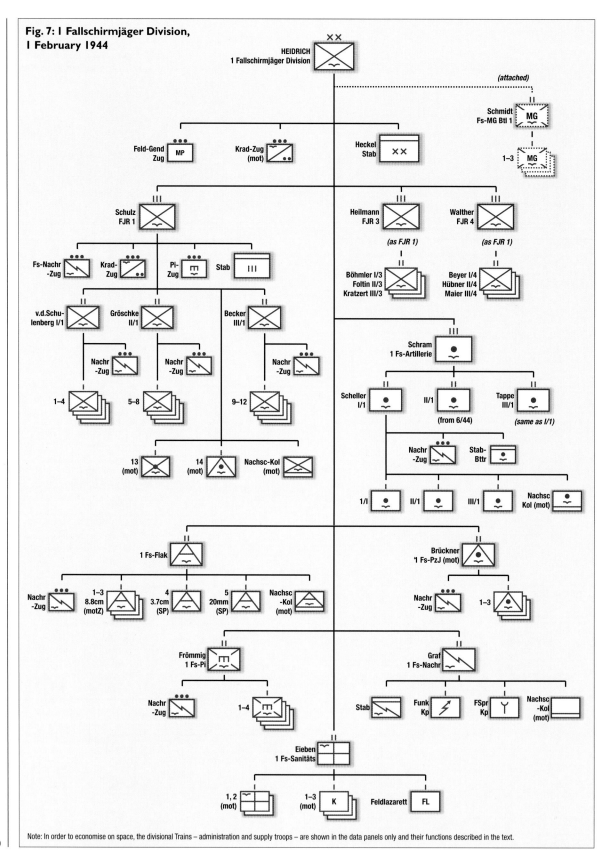

Note: In order to economise on space, the divisional Trains – administration and supply troops – are shown in the data panels only and their functions described in the text.

Fig. 8: 4 Fallschirmjäger Division, 2 June 1944

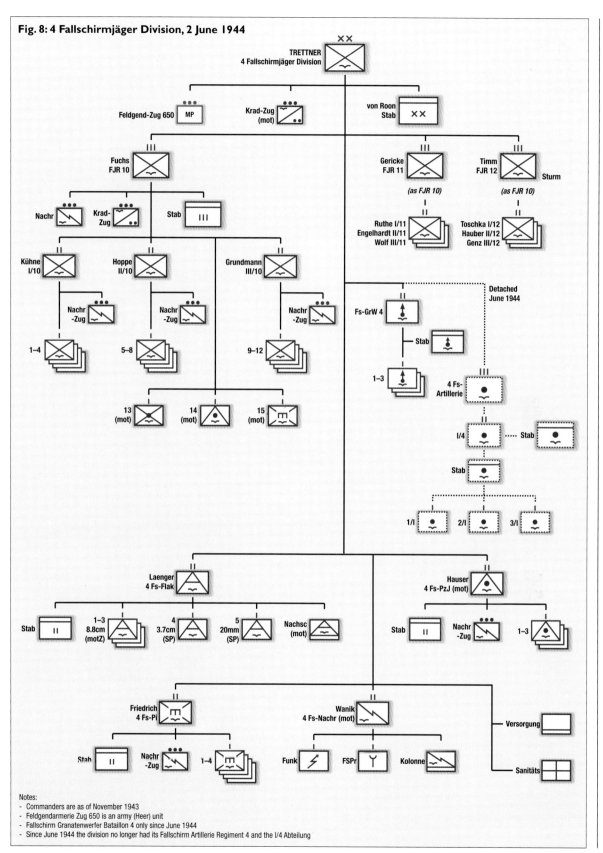

Notes:
- Commanders are as of November 1943
- Feldgendarmerie Zug 650 is an army (Heer) unit
- Fallschirm Granatenwerfer Bataillon 4 only since June 1944
- Since June 1944 the division no longer had its Fallschirm Artillerie Regiment 4 and the I/4 Abteilung

13 Infanteriegeschütz-Kompanie

14 Panzerjäger-Kompanie

Nachschubkolonne (mot)

Fallschirmjäger Regiment 4 (FJR 4)

Major Walther/Major Grassmehl (temporary)

Stab

Nachrichten-Zug

Kradschützen-Zug

Pionier-Zug

I/FJR 4 (*Hauptmann Beyer*)

    1–3 Jäger-Kompanien

    4 Fallschirm-MG-Kompanie

II/FJR 4 (*Hauptmann Hübner*)

    5–7 Jäger-Kompanien

    8 Fallschirm-MG-Kompanie

III/FJR 4 (*Hauptmann Maier*)

    9–11 Jäger-Kompanien

    12 Fallschirm-MG-Kompanie

13 Infanteriegeschütz-Kompanie

14 Panzerjäger-Kompanie

Nachschubkolonne (mot)

Fallschirm-Artillerie Regiment 1 (FAR 1)

Major Bruno Schram

I/FAR 1 (*Major Scheller*)

    Stabsbatterie

    Nachrichten-Zug

    1–3 Batterien

    Nachschub-Kolonne (mot)

II/FAR 1 (*Hauptmann Tappe*)

    Stabsbatterie

    Nachrichten-Zug

    1–3 Batterien

    Nachschub-Kolonne (mot)

Fallschirm-Panzerjäger Abteilung 1 (*Major Brückner*)

    Stab

    Nachrichten-Zug

    1–3 PaK Kompanien

Fallschirm-Flak Abteilung 1

    Stab

(continued on page 43)

Nachrichten-Zug

1–3 schwere Batterien (motZ)

4 mittlere Batterie auf sfl

5 mittlere Batterie auf sfl

Nachschub-Kolonne (mot)

Fallschirm-Pionier Bataillon 1 (*Hauptmann Frömming*)

Stab

Nachrichten-Zug

1–4 Pionier-Kompanien

Fallschirm-Luftnachrichten Abteilung 1 (*Hauptmann Graf*)

Stab

1 Funk-Kompanie

2 Fernsprech-Kompanie

Nachschubkolonne (mot)

Fallschirm-Sanitäts Abteilung 1 (*Obersfeldarzt Dr. Eieben*)

1–2 Sanitäts-Kompanien (mot)

Fallschirm-Feldlzarett 1

1–3 Krankentransport-Kompanien

Divisional Trains:

Fallschirm-Division Nachschubführer (mot) (supply HQ)

Nachschub-Kompanie (mot) (supply company)

Grosse Kraftwagenkolonne für Betriebstoff (mot) (heavy fuel column)

Grosse Kraftwagenkolonne (mot) (heavy supply column)

1–4 leichte Kraftwagenkolonnen (mot) (light supply columns)

1–2 Werkstattkompanie (mot) (maintenance companies)

Divisions-Verwaltungs-Abteilung (mot) (divisional administration detachment)

Bächerei-Kompanie (mot) (bakery company)

Schlachterei-Kompanie (mot) (butcher company)

Feldpostamt (mot) (field post office)

Although 1 Fallschirmjäger Division had received orders to move to Cassino at the end of January, it had in the meantime sent Kampfgruppe 'Schulz' to Anzio. In early February this was moved to Cassino, where III/FJR 4 soon joined it: the vanguard of the division. On 15–18 February Kamfpgruppe 'Schulz' (I, II/FJR 1, III/FJR 3, Fallschirm-MG Bataillon 1) was deployed at Cassino, and it suffered heavy losses while fighting against the 4th Indian Division. When the second battle of Cassino was over, three battalions out of five of Kampfgruppe 'Schulz' had been 'worn out', while two companies of III/FJR 3 had lost all their officers and one fifth of other ranks.

These two images complete the series started on page 38. At top, Italian soldiers of the Royal Italian Army, fighting with the Allies, search a rather disgruntled Fallschirmjäger in a clearly staged photo. At bottom, the two Fallschirmjäger along with two Caucasians, possibly soldiers from the 162 'Turk' Division or simply Hiwis (Hilfswillige, voluntary auxiliaries) from 1 or 4 Fallschirmjäger Division. (Archivio Ufficio Storico Stato Maggiore Esercito (AUSSME) – via Filippo Cappellano)

The rest of 1 Fallschirmjäger Division was in place by 26 February, replacing 90 Panzergrenadier Division between Cassino (FJR 3) and Monastery Hill (FJR 4), while FJR 1, having suffered many losses, was put in reserve to the north. The divisional combat strength was now at 2,805, and most of the battalions had about 200 men: II/FJR 1 had 150, III/FJR 1 had 50 (the whole regiment was 660 strong); FJR 3 was in no better shape with 800 men, II/FJR 3 only had 70, while FJR 4 had 1,160 men. Fallschirm-MG Bataillon was down to 185 men. That did not prevent the German High Command from diluting its strength even further; since 5 Fallschirmjäger Division was forming in France, 1 Fallschirmjäger Division had to provide cadres for it. In April the division handed over III/FJR 1 (used to form FJR 14), III/FJR 3 (used to form FJR 13) and III/FJR 4 (used to form FJR 15). New battalions were raised in Germany, but they did not rejoin 1 Fallschirmjäger Division until June along with the new III/FAR

1, which had been formed in Germany as well (in the same month the 'old' III/FAR 1 was renamed II/FAR 1). Even 4 Fallschirmjäger Division had to make sacrifices, and in June 1944 it handed over I/FAR 4 (the only artillery unit it had) to 6 Fallschirmjäger Division. Although in the same month it was assigned a newly formed Fallschirm-Granatenwerfer Bataillon 4 (with three companies), it was never assigned the newly formed Fallschirm-Artillerie Regiment 4, which was used elsewhere. For the rest of the war the division fought without its own artillery.

The third battle of Cassino, 15–22 March, put a further strain on 1 Fallschirmjäger Division's resources, and it lost 1,378 men. Although a series of army units were attached to the division in May (Fig. 9, below, and Table 5,

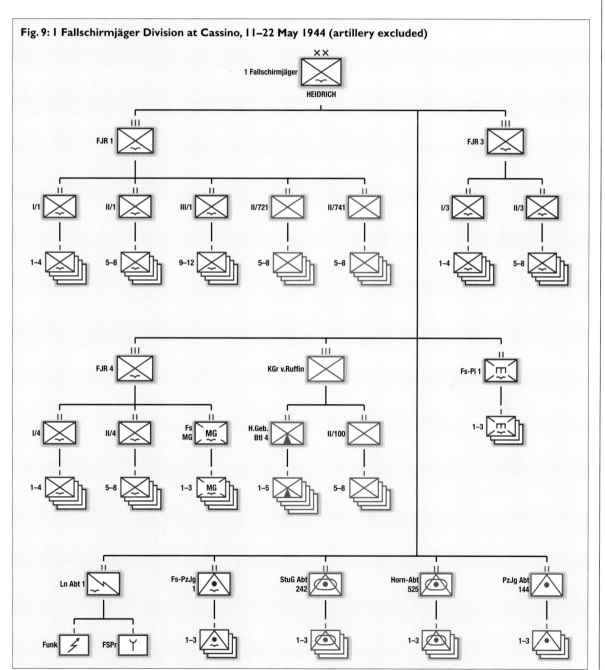

Fig. 9: 1 Fallschirmjäger Division at Cassino, 11–22 May 1944 (artillery excluded)

Gotha Go 242 and Go 244

Once the DFS 230 assault glider had proven itself in combat in Belgium in May 1940, the Gotha design team began looking into ways of improving the concept. What emerged was both a very advanced and very unusual design that has subsequently been emulated many times.

The Go 242, which first flew early in 1941, had the shoulder-mounted wing common to most gliders but was innovative in that it had a twin-boom tail assembly while the central fuselage pod incorporated a 'crocodile jaw' upward hinging rear tail door and downward hinging ramp for bulky loads, as well as a conventional personnel door on the port side. Its main wingspan was not much more than that of the DFS 230 at 24.5m but the extra lift created by the tail span enabled it to carry a weight of 3,900kg compared to a mere 1,240kg. The fuselage itself was 4.56m longer (including the hinged tail) allowing the Go 242A-2 to carry 21 paratroops plus a crew of two – more than the capacity of a Ju 52! The A-1 was a 'freight train' without seating that could carry a Kubelwagen or a Ketten-Krad plus PaK 36 or Flak 38.

A total of 1,528 Go 242s was built, of which 133 were retrospectively fitted with a pair of French Gnome/Rhône 14M engines and designated Go 244. A further 43 machines were new-built as Go 244s and a small number of these were delivered to KGrzbV 104 in Greece and KGrzbV 106 on Crete in March 1942. The Go 242As and Bs issued to XI Fliegerkorps principally went to LLG 1 and 2, most of the remainder going to I-6.VI/KG 200. The gliders were only used in the airborne assault role twice, once during the deployment to Sicily in July 1943 and then again a year later against a Resistance uprising in southern France shortly after D-Day. While some aircraft were used in North Africa and in ferrying supplies to the Greek islands, the majority served in Russia.

Table 5: 1 Fallschirmjäger Division (Heidrich)		
Fallschirmjäger Regiment 1	I/1	1–4
	II/1	5–8
	III/1 *	9–12
	II/721 (114 Jäger Div)	5–8
	II/741 (114 Jäger Div)	5–8
Fallschirmjäger Regiment 3	I/3	1–4
	II/3	5–8
Fallschirmjäger Regiment 4	I/4	1–4
	II/4	5–8
	Fallschirm-MG Bataillon	1–3
Kampfgruppe von Ruffin	Hoch-Gebirgsjäger Bataillon 4	1–5
	II/100 (5 Gebirgs Div)	5–8
Fallschirm-Pioniere Bataillon 1		1–3
Fallschirm-Panzerjäger Abteilung 1		1–3
Luftnachrichten-Abteilung 1		1 (Funk)–2 (Fernspräch)
Sturmgeschütz Abteilung 242		1–3
Panzerjäger-Abteilung 525 ('Hornisse')		1–3
Panzerjäger-Abteilung 144		1–3
* About to leave for Germany in mid-May		

above), both combat losses and the transfer of its units greatly reduced its strength – though not its capabilities, as the Poles were to discover on 11–18 May during the fourth battle of Cassino. When the division finally withdrew, its combat strength was less than 1,000: FJR 4 had 235 men, FJR 3 had 238, FJR 1 had 349 and Fallschirm-Pionier Bataillon 1 only had 72 men. For both 1 and 4 Fallschirmjäger Divisions the slow withdrawal to northern Italy had begun. On 3 June, 1 Fallschirmjäger Division was north-west of Rome at Tivoli, moving north along the Tiber Valley following the route Orvieto–Arezzo (Fig. 10, page 47) until, in September, it reached Rimini, where it fought another bloody battle. After a desperate attempt to slow down the American advance in front of Rome, 4 Fallschirmjäger Division (the last German unit to leave the Eternal City on 4 June) withdrew north along the route Viterbo–Siena–Firenze, eventually halting the Allied advance at the Futa Pass.

Both divisions fought hard in the positions of the Gothic Line during the winter of 1944/45. In November 1944 Heidrich took over command of I Fallschirm-Korps from Schlemm, and he was replaced by Schulz as comander of 1 Fallschirmjäger Division. In December both divisions were assigned their Fallschirm-Feldersatz Bataillon (1 with five companies, 4 with four), while in March 1945 4 Fallschirmjäger Division had to hand over II/FJR 12 and 2/Fallschirm-Pionier Bataillon 4 for the formation of 10 Fallschirmjäger Division in Austria. In April 1945 both 1 and 2 Fallschirmjäger Divisions were near Bologna and, after the Allied offensive, withdrew north toward the Brenner Pass. Both suffered heavy losses during the crossing of the Po River, and their remnants eventually surrendered to American forces on 2 May 1945. The Italian campaign was over.

Fig. 10: 1 Fallschirmjäger Division, 1 July 1944

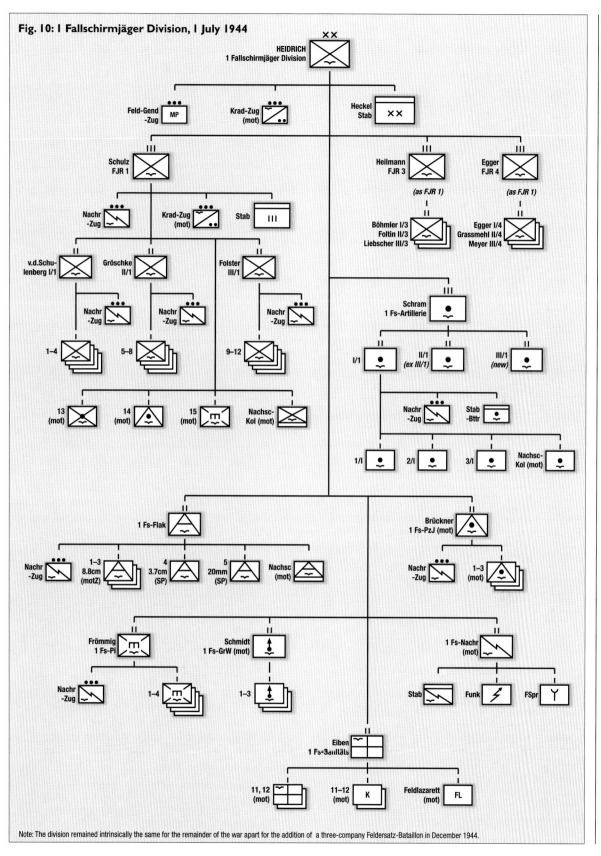

Note: The division remained intrinsically the same for the remainder of the war apart for the addition of a three-company Feldersatz-Bataillon in December 1944.

Unit organization (3):

185° Divisione Paracadutisti 'Folgore', 184° 'Nembo' and 183° 'Ciclone'

with Pier Paolo Battistelli

Although the inclusion of a special section on Italian paratroopers may seem odd in a book about German airborne divisions, there are three specific reasons. First, the Italian army (Regio Esercito) of World War II has always received a bad press, which in the case of the paras is totally undeserved. Second, the Paracadutisti fought alongside the Fallschirmtruppe at El Alamein, on Sicily and in southern Italy, while after the armistice in September 1943 a significant number elected to continue fighting for the Axis, hundreds being ultimately absorbed into XI Fliegerkorps, 2 and the new 4 Fallschirmjäger Divisions, and I Fallschirmkorps. Thirdly, despite the existence of two full and one incomplete Italian parachute divisions, an airlanding division and a miscellany of smaller formations, there is such a paucity of reliable documentary information on them in English that it is hoped this sketch will go some way towards rectifying the situation.

The Italians were first in the field to experiment seriously with paratroops in 1917, and an assault company under Tenente (Lieutenant) Alessandro Tandura was dropped across the river Piave during the battle of Vittorio Veneto in October the following year. However, although the concept was not abandoned, it then languished until Russian demonstrations revived interest in the early 1930s. Even so, little more constructive was done other than a shortlived decision taken in 1937 that any future parachute forces should fall under the command of the Regia Aeronautica rather than the Regio Esercito, just as the Fallschirmjäger would come under the Luftwaffe rather than the Heer. As in Germany, there were widespread misgivings about the whole idea, although given their origins it was thought that paratroops might be useful for sabotage operations behind enemy lines, particularly

Italian paratroopers of the 'Folgore' Division line up at Tarquinia airport to have their parachutes checked before a training jump. Note the jump smock and gear, clearly inspired by German patterns. A camouflage smock was also produced. (Archivio Ufficio Storico Stato Maggiore Esercito (AUSSME) – via Filippo Cappellano)

against C3I assets. By 1937, of course, Italian forces were already fighting on General Francisco Franco's side in Spain and had successfully occupied Abyssinia (Ethiopia) the year before, while plans were being drawn up for an invasion of Albania.

A key figure in the creation of the future Italian airborne corps was the governor-general of Libya, Maresciallo dell'Aria (Air Marshal) Italo Balbo – like Kurt Student, a former World War I fighter pilot – who commanded the Forze Armate dell'Africa Settentrionale (North African Armed Forces). Foreseeing that his future military operations were most likely to take place against the British and/or the French in North Africa, Balbo decided that the terrain here would generally be suitable for the deployment of paratroops on a larger scale than merely as commandos. In this he had the support of the then army chief of staff (Stato Maggiore), Generale Alberto Pariani, who had his own eye on an invasion of Egypt and regarded airborne forces as a potential means of catching the British off balance and diverting their reserves while the main overland assault went in.

On 22 March 1938 Balbo began assembling native volunteers (Ascari) under Italian officers for 1° Battaglione Fanti dell'Aria Libici – 1st Libyan Airborne Infantry Battalion – which was commanded by Tenente-Colonnello (Lieutenant-Colonel) Goffredo Tonini. Shortly afterwards Balbo also established a training school at Castel Benito airfield just outside Tripoli, the parachute programme being entrusted to Tenente Prospero Freri. The battalion was first dropped en masse during manoeuvres at Bir al Ghnem on 16 April, but 15 men were killed so the old D/37 'Salvatore' (Saviour) parachute was replaced as quickly as possible by the Modello I/40, which had a larger canopy. Despite this setback, within a year Balbo had begun formation of a second battalion, again from native troops, but this was disbanded in favour of raising an ethnic Italian parachute battalion instead. The 1° Battaglione Fanti dell'Aria Nazionali mustered on 23 May 1940 under Maggiore (Major) Arturo Calascibetta, just before Mussolini's declaration of war against England and France on 10 June. Neither the Libyan nor the Italian battalion numbered more than about 300 officers and men. Meanwhile, on 13 October 1939 the army had opened a rival parachute school at Tarquinia, near the coast north-west of Rome, under Colonnello Giuseppe Baudoin de Gillette, but again there was no real development until 1940.

In spring 1942 the 'Folgore' Division began training for the planned attack against Malta. The major training area was around Tarquinia in northern Lazio. Here a column of paratroopers passes by General Ugo Cavallero, Chief of the Italian General Staff. (Archivio Ufficio Storico Stato Maggiore Esercito (AUSSME) – via Filippo Cappellano)

Unfortunately for the air force parachute battalions in Libya, Balbo was killed shortly after the start of hostilities when his aircraft was shot down by 'friendly' flak over Tobruk on 28 June. His successor, Maresciallo Rodolfo Graziani, lacked aggression and none of the paras were used at all during the invasion of Egypt he launched reluctantly on 13 September. After only reaching as far east as Sidi Barâni, Graziani halted his advance, passing the initiative to the British. When Lieutenant-General Richard O'Connor's Western Desert Force began its spirited counteroffensive on 8 December, the Italian troops fell back in disorder. There is an unsubstantiated claim from this period that during the retreat a forward airstrip (location unspecified) was abandoned and that a squad from the original Libyan battalion was air-dropped to sabotage the aircraft left behind, before themselves retiring on foot to Tobruk. Better authenticated is the fact that two battalions were thrown into action, though not parachuted, as a battlegroup (Raggruppamento) under Colonnello Tonini at Derna on 15 January 1941 to help cover the withdrawal of 10° Armata from Cyrenaica into Tripolitania. This rearguard action was at least partially successful but the majority of the surviving paratroops were finally overwhelmed and taken prisoner at Beda Fomm on 7 February.

Back at Tarquinia, the Regio Esercito had taken tentative steps towards the creation of what would eventually become the first Italian airborne division, 'Folgore' (Thunderbolt, named from its motto 'Ex alto fulgor'). The original battalion 'Tuscania' under Maggiore Bruto Bersanetti was recruited from the Carabinieri for much the same reasons as the initial German paratroop formation came from the Polizei. The first 50 volunteers assembled in Rome on 10 July 1940 and began parachute training three days later. When complete, the battalion consisted of 22 officers, 50 NCOs and 320 men in three companies. A second battalion was then recruited from the infantry (Fanteria) under Tenente-Colonnello Benzi and a third from the Regia Aeronautica under Maggiore Pignatelli de Cherciara; by November these constituted the provisional Brigata Paracadutisti 'Folgore' with Colonnello Riccardo Bignami as Chef. The drop-out rate during training was 60 per cent, so those who completed Baudoin's rigorous two-month programme rightly considered themselves an elite. Maggiore Bechi Luserna's fourth battalion from the Cavalleria, plus the survivors from Raggruppamento 'Tonini', joined them on 31 March 1941; and on 10 August a battalion (Gruppo) of artillerymen from the Alpini equipped with 75mm Ansaldo M35 pack howitzers was attached. Like the weapons originally issued to 7 Flieger Division, these could be broken down into seven or eight components for parachute drops although this was never actually done in a war situation.

A group of paratroopers assembling soon after their landing during an exercise in Tarquinia in spring 1942. Training for the 'Folgore' Division was partly inspired by German Fallschirmjäger commanders, producing one of the most well-trained Italian Army units as was shown at the battle of El Alamein. (Archivio Ufficio Storico Stato Maggiore Esercito (AUSSME) – via Filippo Cappellano)

As in the case of the original 7 Flieger Division, the 'Folgore' Brigade benefited from a wide variety of talent and experience, but only a handful of its members ever made a combat jump. This took place at the end of the Greek campaign on 30 April 1941, when 80 men from the 5° and 6° Compagnie of II Battaglione Paracadutisti under Capitini Avogadro and Macchiato were dropped to secure the island of Cephalonia – the setting for the film *Captain Corelli's Mandolin*. The aircraft used were Savoia-Marchetti SM 81s from 56° Gruppo da Bombardamento then based at Gadurra in Greece. The paras' radio landed in the sea and several men broke limbs in heavy falls on the rocky ground, but the 250-strong police garrison capitulated without firing a shot as the Greek government had already surrendered and King George II of the Hellenes had evacuated to Crete. After this, like most of the Fallschirmjäger, the Italian paras would solely find themselves deployed as ordinary infantry. First to suffer in this role was I Battaglione Paracadutisti 'Tuscania', now under Maggiore Edoardo Alessi, which was despatched to help Rommel in July; it was almost completely destroyed at Agedabia in early December during Lieutenant-General Sir Alan Cunningham's Operation Crusader.

In the interim, Bignami's parachute brigade at Tarquinia was reconstituted officially on 1 September as 1° Divisione Paracadutisti 'Folgore' under Generale Francesco Sapienza. With the air/sea invasion of Malta specifically in mind, it soon had three infantry regiments (1°–3°) of 1,482 men apiece, plus a 459-man parachute-saboteur (guastatori-paracadutisti) battalion under Maggiore Burzi modelled on Sturmabteilung 'Koch'. Two months later, on 15 November, an airlanding (Aereotrasportabile) division was formed at Pisa for the same purpose: Generale Gavino Pizzolato's 80° Divisione di Fanteria. It was originally given the name 'Spezia' (Spice), but this produced such ribaldry that it was hastily changed to 'La Spézia' after the nearby city. It only had two infantry regiments, 125° and 126°, plus 80° Reggimento Artigliera and 80° Esplorante (reconnaissance), Controcarri (anti-tank) and Misto Genio (mixed engineer) Battaglioni; the engineer battalion included signallers (Tele/Radiotelegrafisti), and there were also small medical (Sanità), supply (Sussistenza) and MT (Trasporti) sections. Total strength was 6,994 officers and men.

A lonely kneeling paracadutista looks around, still wearing his jump harness, in a clearly staged photo. He is holding a model 91/38 7.35mm rifle with a folding bayonet. It was not a very good weapon, though it suited the requirements of airborne troops. (Archivio Ufficio Storico Stato Maggiore Esercito (AUSSME) – via Filippo Cappellano)

Fig. 11: Axis order of battle for the planned assault on Malta, May 1942

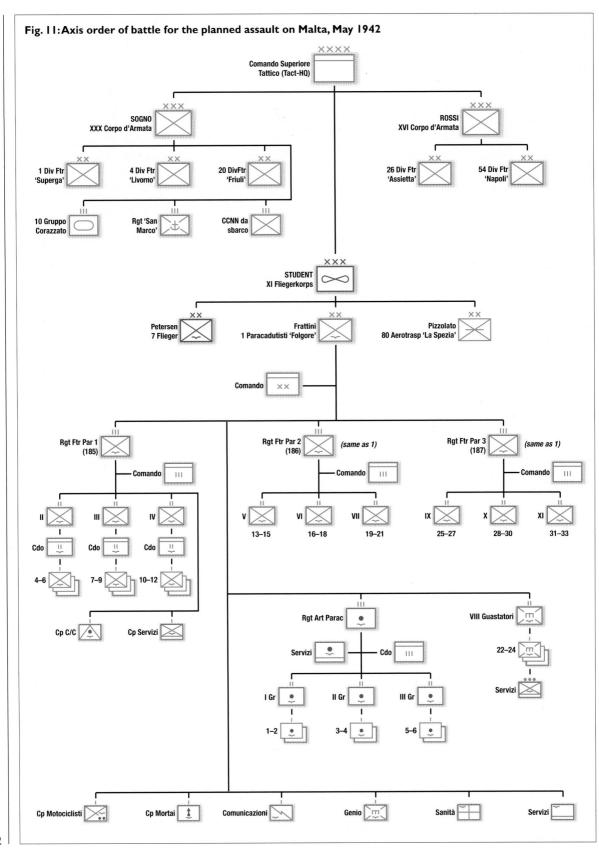

Table 6: Axis order of battle for the planned assault on Malta, May 1942
Corpo d'Armata d'Aviosbarco
General der Flieger Kurt Student (Airborne assault wave)
7 Flieger Division (-) (Ramcke)
1° Divisione Paracadutisti 'Folgore' (Frattini)
80° Divisione Aereotrasportabile 'La Spézia' (Pizzolato)
XXX Corpo d'Armata
Generale Vittorio Sogno (First seaborne assault wave)
1° Divisione di Fanteria 'Superga'
4° Divisione di Fanteria 'Livorno'
20° Divisione di Fanteria 'Friuli'
10° Gruppo Corazzato
Reggimento Fanteria di Marina 'San Marco'
Gruppo Camicie Nere da Sbarco
XVI Corpo d'Armata
Generale Mario Rossi (Second seaborne wave)
26° Divisione di Fanteria 'Assietta'
54° Divisione di Fanteria 'Napoli'

'Folgore' itself was further expanded during the winter of 1941–42 as shown below, although I Battaglione 'Tuscania' was never rebuilt. On 1 March Generale Enrico Frattini[5] took command of the paras, and both 'Folgore' and 'La Spézia' began training in earnest for the proposed Maltese operation. They benefited from the loan of Fallschirmjäger instructors under the supervision of Bernhard Ramcke, all of whom had seen action on Crete and therefore had a heightened understanding of the type of difficulties that were certain to be encountered. Beaches, DZs and airfields on Corsica were used extensively for rehearsals, well away from Allied observation. The Italian codename for the operation was C3 and overall commander was to have been Generale Vittorio Sogno. Whether or not it could have succeeded is endlessly debatable but if it had it might significantly have affected the course of the war. The forces to have been deployed, totalling circa 35,000 men in the assault waves, were as displayed. (Fig. 11, page 52, and Table 6, above)

By the end of March Frattini had incorporated the assault battalion into the third 'Folgore' regiment so that the division now comprised 1° Reggimento Paracadutisti (II, III and IV Battaglioni), 2° Reggimento (V, VI and VII Battaglioni), 3° Reggimento (VIII Guastatori, IX, X and XI Battaglioni), 1° Reggimento Artigliera Paracadutisti (I–III Gruppi, each with eight air-portable 47mm L/32 guns in two batteries), a mortar company (Compagnia Mortai) with 12 81mm tubes, a motorcycle company (Compagnia Motociclisti) with 102 bikes, a mixed engineer company and small medical and supply sections.

These were not the only paratroops who would have been involved in Operation C3, however. Also vital to success was the elite 'San Marco' Reggimento di Marina with its 200-year-old traditions. Its original wartime battalions 'Bafile' and 'Grado', each of about 500 men, would have been necessary, as would its parachute-swimmers (nuotatori-paracadutisti) who

---

5 Frattini, an officer of engineers, was something of an Italian national hero and postwar became C-in-C NATO Forces
Southern Europe.

German and Italian officers inspecting the Parachute Training School at Tarquinia in 1942. Second from left is General Kurt Student (the one on the right could be either Ramcke or von Richthofen). The school was founded on 15 October 1939 and, though an Air Force establishment, it was widely used by the Army to train both the 'Folgore' and 'Nembo' divisions. (Archivio Ufficio Storico Stato Maggiore Esercito (AUSSME) – via Filippo Cappellano)

foreshadowed the US Navy SEALs; and the attached two companies of the naval Camicie Nere Milmart organization. Throughout the war, the Forza Navale Speciale made a successful speciality of unconventional raiding methods including the use of 'frogmen', 'chariots', inflatable dinghies and small high-speed powerboats. The paras were an addition who by 14 October 1942 had grown into the HQ and three rifle companies of the 260-man 'San Marco' Battaglione Paracadutisti. The first 40 volunteers had enrolled at Tarquinia on 22 March 1941, but by 30 May 1942 they still only numbered 140 divided into an HQ and six teams that would have been used to clear the Maltese landing beaches of mines and other obstacles for XXX Corpo. In the event, of course, the invasion of Malta was eventually called off at the beginning of July, something Italian historians are rather scathing about.

One consequence was that 'Folgore' lost its unique status and on 27 July, renumbered 185° Divisione Paracadutisti as a 'binary' division (see below), was sent to join first X Corpo d'Armata, then XX, then X again in Egypt. (Frattini additionally commanded X Corpo up to 26 October.) By this time its regiments had also been renumbered 185°–187°, while the battalions were reshuffled twice, finally giving III, VIII Guastatori and XI to 185° Reggimento, V, VI and VII to 186° and II, IV, IX and X to 187°. At Alamein, however, VII and VIII Battaglioni were brigaded together as Raggruppamento 'Ruspoli'. Each regiment now included its own mortar company with six 81mm tubes and an infantry gun company (Compagnia da 47/32) with six of the ubiquitous dual-purpose 47mm guns. (Fig. 12, page 56)

Despite their shortcomings, 12 instead of the earlier eight of these weapons now also equipped each of the three battalions (I–III Gruppi) in Colonnello Ernesto Boffa's 185° Reggimento Artigliera Paracadutisti. This made the 'regiment' the mere equivalent of a German anti-tank battalion, and it only had 577 men, but it was considerably reinforced in Egypt by attachments from other units and was the only component of the division to be fully motorized. The attachments included two truck-mounted self-propelled 'fast' (Celere) battalions and two towed battalions of 75mm L/27 field guns; a heavy battalion with 100mm L/17 howitzers; and two companies of 20mm L/35 anti-aircraft guns. The 'Folgore' Division also included engineer, signals, medical and supply elements, plus an MT section that only had enough trucks to carry three platoons! Overall strength was 84 officers, 443 NCOs and 5,732 ORs (excluding the artillery attachments), of whom around 4,500 were actually paratroopers.

The paras in the infantry battalions were obviously the principal combat component of the division. Each, with the exception of VIII Guastatori, consisted of 494 officers, NCOs and men with 40 pistols, 360 rifles/carbines and 54 sub-machine guns, excluding the weapons in the support platoon. The basic 'building block' was the squad of one NCO and eight enlisted men, dictated by the carrying capacity of the Savoia-Marchetti SM81. Senior NCOs carried 9mm Beretta M38 or M38/42 sub-machine guns but the majority of the ORs had 7.35mm Mannlicher-Carcano M38 carbines; each squad also included one 6.5mm Breda Modello 30 light machine gun (Fucile Mitragliatore). Three squads formed a 27-man section led by a sergeant, and two sections a 54–55-man platoon commanded by a lieutenant. Three platoons constituted a company under its captain, giving an average total of 164–168 personnel. (Officers wore 7.65mm or 9mm Beretta M34 or 7.65mm M35 pistols.) For tactical support each company included a 40-man heavy machine-gun (Mitragliatrice) platoon with four 8mm Breda Modello 37s, six light 45mm mortars, six anti-tank rifles and six flamethrowers. VIII Guastatori Battaglione only had 459 personnel – 34 officers, 31 NCOs and 394 men – but a greater variety of support weaponry and equipment including, for example, bangalore torpedoes to blast holes through barbed wire. (Fig. 12, page 56, and Table 7, below)

Table 7: 185° Divisione Paracadutisti 'Folgore', 23 October 1942

(Note: Only those units present at Alamein listed)

Generale Enrico Frattini

Stato Maggiore Colonnello Riccardo Bignami

9° Squadriglia Pilotaggio ('flight deck' squadron for liaison and reconnaissance)

185° Sezione Mista Carabinieri (MP section)

260° Ufficio Postale (Post Office)

185° Reggimento Paracadutisti (-)

VIII Battaglione Guastatori (brigaded with VII/186°) (*Maggiore Burzi*)

    22, 23 & 24 Compagnie

186° Reggimento Paracadutisti

Colonnello Tantillo

V Battaglione (*Maggiore Izzo*)

    13, 14 & 15 Compagnie

VI Battaglione (*Maggiore Bersonzi*)

    16, 17 & 18 Compagnie

VII Battaglione (brigaded with VIII/185°) (*Tenente-Colonnello Ruspoli*)

    19, 20 & 21 Compagnie

(continued on page 57)

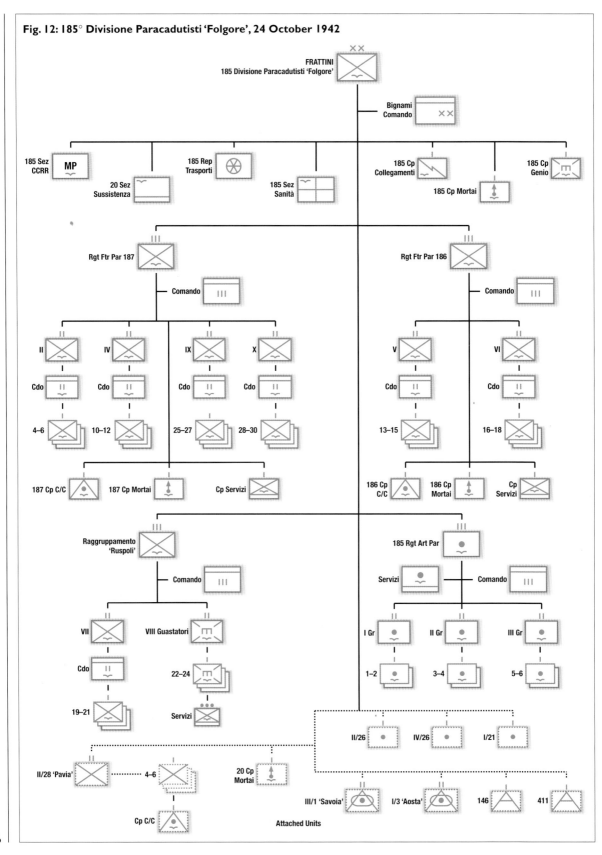

Fig. 12: 185° Divisione Paracadutisti 'Folgore', 24 October 1942

FRATTINI
185 Divisione Paracadutisti 'Folgore'

Bignami
Comando

185 Sez CCRR
MP

20 Sez Sussistenza

185 Rep Trasporti

185 Sez Sanità

185 Cp Collegamenti

185 Cp Mortai

185 Cp Genio

Rgt Ftr Par 187

Comando

Rgt Ftr Par 186

Comando

II

IV

IX

X

V

VI

Cdo

Cdo

Cdo

Cdo

Cdo

Cdo

4–6

10–12

25–27

28–30

13–15

16–18

187 Cp C/C

187 Cp Mortai

Cp Servizi

186 Cp C/C

186 Cp Mortai

Cp Servizi

Raggruppamento 'Ruspoli'

Comando

185 Rgt Art Par

Servizi

Comando

VII

VIII Guastatori

I Gr

II Gr

III Gr

Cdo

22–24

1–2

3–4

5–6

19–21

Servizi

II/26

IV/26

I/21

II/28 'Pavia'

4–6

20 Cp Mortai

III/1 'Savoia'

I/3 'Aosta'

146

411

Cp C/C

Attached Units

56

186° Compagnia da 47/32 (one platoon detached to Raggruppamento 'Ruspoli')
186° Compagnia Mortai da 81

187° Reggimento Paracadutisti

Colonnello Camosso
II Battaglione (*Maggiore Zanninovich*)
4 & 5 Compagnie (6° detached)
IV Battaglione (*Tenente-Colonnello Luserno*)
10, 11 & 12 Compagnie
IX Battaglione (-) (*Maggiore Rossi*)
25, 26 & 27 Compagnie
X Battaglione (*Capitano Carugno*)
28, 29 & 30 Compagnie
187° Compagnia da 47/32
187° Compagnia Mortai da 81

185° Reggimento Artigliera Paracadutisti

Colonello Boffa
I Gruppo
1 & 2 Batterie (each 6 x 47/32)
II Gruppo
3 & 4 Batterie (ditto)
III Gruppo
5 & 6 Batterie (ditto)

185° Compagnia Mortai da 81 Divisionale (18 x 81mm?)*
146° Compagnia Contraereo (8 x 20/35; one source says only 6)
411° Compagnia Contraereo (ditto)
III/1° Gruppo Celere Eugenio di Savoia (from Corps Reserve) (12 x 75/27 SP)
I/3° Gruppo Celere Duca D'Aosta (from Corps Reserve) (ditto)
II/ & IV/26° Gruppi Rubicone (attached from Pavia Division) (each 12 x 75/27 towed)
I/21° Gruppo Po (attached from Trieste Division) (12 x 100/17)
185° Compagnia Comunicazioni
3 Plotoni
185° Compagnia Minatori/Artieri (12 x flamethrowers)
3 Plotoni
185° Sezione Sanità
185° Reparto Trasporti
20° Batteria Mortai da 45 (6 x 45mm)*
20° Sezione Sussistenza

* *20° Batteria is shown in one source as having been absorbed by 185° Compagnia, which may account for the unusual figure of 18 mortars in the latter although not all were 81mm.*

During the battle of El Alamein, holding the line deep on the southern flank with the Ramcke Brigade further to their north, the Italian paras helped bring Lieutenant-General Brian Horrocks' XIII Corps (including 7th Armoured Division) to a standstill but, lacking motor transport, most of the survivors – including Frattini and Bignami – were unable to escape and eventually captured after Montgomery broke through to their north (Operation Supercharge). The division was beaten by logistics, and remained undefeated in battle, but was still officially disbanded on 23 November. (A similar fate awaited 'La Spézia' six months later in Tunisia.) All that escaped of 'Folgore' was a small composite battalion, later renumbered XII, which by April 1943 was down to a mere 200 men.

However, 'Folgore' had been designated a binary division, meaning that it was going to be used to spawn a second parachute division, and two full battalions, III/ and XI/185° Reggimento, plus the 185° regimental staff and the motorcycle company, had remained in Italy while the rest of the division went to Africa. On 1 November they found themselves forming the nucleus of 184° Divisione Paracadutisti 'Nembo' (Stormcloud) under Generale Ercole Ronco, based originally in Pisa. Moved to Florence in December, on 1 January 1943 'Nembo' found itself designated a ternary division! Thus, although it had been further stripped before Alamein when the bulk of XI Battaglione was despatched to Egypt to replace casualties, it was joined by reconstituted XI and VIII Battaglioni plus two further infantry regiments raised during the winter of 1942–43, numbered 183° Reggimento Fanteria Paracadutista (reconstituted X plus new XV and XVI Battaglioni) and 184° (XIII and XIV); plus 184° Reggimento Artigliera Paracadutisti (I–III Gruppi), 184° Battaglione Guastatori, 184° Compagnia Mortai, 184° Compagnia Motociclisti, 284° Compagnia Ciclisti, 184° Compagnie Genio Artieri, Mista Genio and Tele/Radiotelegrafisti, plus 184° Reparto Trasporti and even 184° Reparto Carristi (tank detachment). However, few, if any, of the latecomers received parachute training at the new school outside Viterbo; neither did the Regia Aeronautica proceed with an assault glider, the Caproni TM2, after the prototype crashed.

In the spring of 1943, still commanded by Ronco, the 'Nembo' Division was despatched to Gorizia near the north-east Adriatic coast to combat incursions by strong Yugoslav partisan forces. With the final defeat of the Italo-German armies in Tunisia in May, the much more serious threat of an Anglo-American invasion took priority, so in June 183° and 184° Reggimenti were sent to Sardinia where the initial assault was expected (see 'The man who never was', page 17) while 185° went to Calabria – the 'toe' of the Italian 'boot'. 184° Reggimento was also now brought up to three battalions by the addition of Maggiore Mario Rizzatti's composite XII Battaglione evacuated from Tunisia – the last true remnant of 'Folgore'. When the Allies unexpectedly landed on Sicily instead of Sardinia in July, 185° Reggimento was quickly shipped across the Strait of Messina to play a key role fighting as a rearguard while Kesselring evacuated the bulk of the surviving Italian and German troops back to the mainland in August.

Here, the three 'Nembo' battalions (III, VIIII and XI/185°) were deployed alongside FJR 1, II/FJR 4 and other German units against Montgomery's XIII Corps that began landing near Reggio on 3 September – helping to precipitate the Italian capitulation the following week. Under Kesselring's orders to fall back to link up with stronger forces to the north, the paras contented themselves by only offering enough resistance in the Aspromonte massif to cause enemy casualties. When the Allies then forced the Italian hand by broadcasting news of the impending armistice on 8 September – only hours before the American Fifth Army landing at Salerno – German troops moved in a pre-arranged plan to disarm, and in many cases massacre, their erstwhile allies. Thousands of Italian soldiers, left without orders, simply deserted and vanished into the countryside while those who delayed through indecision usually regretted it when they ended up in German labour camps. Amongst the paratroops and many other units, however, a substantial number of men – perhaps 150,000 overall –

decided to continue the struggle for the Axis and 'per l'onore d'Italia' in Mussolini's new Repubblica Sociale Italiana (RSI), formed on 23 September after his rescue from Gran Sasso. They included almost the whole of Rizatti's XII/184° Battaglione on Sardinia, which mutinied and shot the chief of staff of the 'Nembo' Division, and one and a half companies from Maggiore Massimino's III/185° Battaglione in Calabria, led by Capitano Edoardo Sala; plus most of Capitano Alfredo Busoli's fledgling XX Battaglione 'Azzurro' (Azure). This was one of three new training (Allievi) battalions – XVII, XVIII and XX – that were in the process of being created in cadre at Tradate just before the armistice as the nucleus for the ternary 183° Divisione Paracadutisti 'Ciclone' (Cyclone). It is with the armistice, the creation of the RSI, the division of the country into north and south and what amounted to civil war that the history of the Paracadutisti unfortunately becomes rather entangled. For example, amongst the first units to re-enlist with the Germans was 112° Compagnia Camionettisti (motorized) from 3° Esplorante Battaglione of the Esercito Nazionale Repubblicano's new 3° Divisione Fanteria di Marina 'San Marco' – which had nothing to do with the Marines, being an army formation and formerly II Battaglione of 10° Arditi Reggimento. This Italian company, in German uniform, went to Rome's Pratica di Mare airfield to swell the ranks of 2 Fallschirmjäger Division's own reconnaissance troops. 122° Compagnia took a similar route and was deployed in coastal defence, but it did not go to Russia with the division.

Even more curious is the 'Decima Mas' saga. This unit began as 10° Flottiglia MAS – a highly successful raiding flotilla equipped with motor torpedo boats from which to launch their human torpedoes. The morning after the armistice, its charismatic CO, Prince Junio Valerio Borghese, collected together every man he

Colonel Giuseppe Baudoin shows the 91/38 rifle to General Student. In 1939, aged 43, he became the first commander of the Parachute Training School of Tarquinia, which he practically created out of nowhere. An infantry officer during World War I, Baudoin became a pilot in the mid-1920s – the perfect prototype of a paratrooper. (Archivio Ufficio Storico Stato Maggiore Esercito (AUSSME) – via Filippo Cappellano)

could in the flotilla's home city, La Spézia, confined them to barracks during the emergency, and drove to see the German garrison commander. He offered the whole Decima Mas organization on a plate – an offer that was received with astonishment but accepted gratefully. Borghese then spent the next two weeks recruiting throughout north Italy until, by the time the RSI came into existence, he had an entire division, the Divisione Fanteria di Marina 'Decima'. Amongst more than two-dozen disparate companies and battalions, it included two companies of nuotatori-paracadutisti and three companies of regular parachutists. To further complicate the issue, the RSI National Guard (Guarda Nazionale Repubblicana) created a new 'Mazzarini' parachute battalion and the Aeronautica Nazionale Repubblicana also decided to get into the act, which was shortly to cause problems for Kurt Student.

After the armistice, most of the former Regia Aeronautica's Battaglione Arditi Distruttori and Regia Marina's small Battaglione Nuotatori Paracadutisti also elected to serve the RSI. (Other men chose the alternative route and volunteered to work with the British, who confusingly designated 185° Reggimento Paracadutisti 'Nembo' as part of Raggruppamenti 'Legnano' or 'Folgore'. The Allied contingents were widely used later in drops to both communist and royalist partisan groups behind German lines.)

Those companies and battalions with any claim to being paras and which had stayed with the Axis cause, however, were initially just allocated to XI Fliegerkorps as a tactical reserve and deployed south of Rome, or in coastal defence duties, while OKW decided what to do with them. Eventually, just before Christmas 1943, Maresciallo Graziani – yes, that Graziani who, despite his dismal record, had wormed his way up to chief of staff to the RSI – asked Kurt Student to raise a new Italian parachute regiment using these and any other volunteers. Student's task was complicated by the fact that on 23 November the new Aeronautica Repubblicana had appropriated 900-odd men

Italian paratroopers from the 'Folgore' Regiment of the RSI gathered together with German Fallschirmjäger and soldiers of the Xᵃ MAS Flotilla to give their last salute to a fallen comrade. (Count E.G. Vitetti collection)

of the former Arditi battalion into a Raggruppamento Paracadutisti at Tradate, and on 1 December a similar number into the Battaglione Arditi Paracadutisti Aeronautica Repubblicana. This left just approximately 750 men of the old XII/184° and III/185° as combat-ready troops plus some of the XX/183° volunteers who were still only partially trained; one contemporary account describes them as 'schoolboys and college students'.

On 25 December – with Kesselring's approval – Student ordered the formation of Graziani's new regiment as part of 'Heinz' Trettner's equally new and still only partially assembled 4 Fallschirmjäger Division. With just 750 men, Student could only form a single battalion, I Battaglione 'Nembo' under Major Kleye with Capitano Corradino Alvino as deputy. It had an original strength of 433 in four understrength companies; apparently the remainder of the men temporarily went to swell the ranks of II/ and III/FJR 10 under Oberst Adolf Fuchs and II/ and III/FJR 12 under Major Erich Timm. They all fought on the Anzio–Nettuno front as part of Richard Heidrich's new I Fallschirmkorps from early February 1944 while Student struggled to get the 1,800-odd men pre-empted by the Aeronautica Repubblica released back to him. He did not succeed until 19 April and the new Reggimento Ardito Paracadutisti 'Folgore' officially came into existence on 1 May, but even then it was not incorporated into 4 Fallschirmjäger Division as Student wished but remained part of the air force, as the planners had originally conceived back in 1937. It had a mixture of German and Italian officers to further confuse the C3I situation! (Fig. 13, below, and Table 8, page 62)

On 27 May the new regiment was deployed to the south-west of Rome, less HQ, 11. and 12./III, which remained at Spoleto. By this stage of the war the need was for men who would remain steady under pressure rather than esoteric skills, and the men fought well until July when appalling losses, particularly amongst the German officers and NCOs, caused their virtual disintegration and

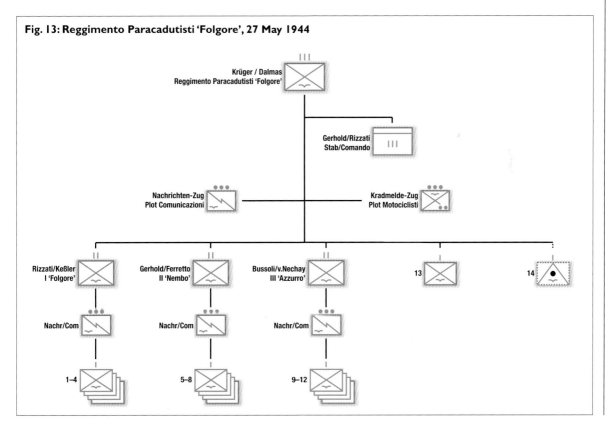

Fig. 13: Reggimento Paracadutisti 'Folgore', 27 May 1944

Krüger / Dalmas
Reggimento Paracadutisti 'Folgore'

Gerhold/Rizzati
Stab/Comando

Nachrichten-Zug
Plot Comunicazioni

Kradmelde-Zug
Plot Motociclisti

Rizzati/Keßler
I 'Folgore'

Gerhold/Ferretto
II 'Nembo'

Bussoli/v.Nechay
III 'Azzurro'

13

14

Nachr/Com

Nachr/Com

Nachr/Com

1–4

5–8

9–12

Table 8: Reggimento Ardito Paracadutisti 'Folgore', 27 May 1944*

Oberstleutnant Adolf Krüger/Colonnello Dalmas

Ia: *Hauptmann Hans Gerhold/Maggiore Mario Rizzati*

Nachrichten-Zug/Plotone Comunicazioni

Kradmelde-Zug/Plotone Motociclisti

I Bataillon/Battaglione 'Folgore'

Maggiore Mario Rizzati/Hauptmann Keßler

Nachrichten-Zug/Plotone Comunicazioni

    1–4 Kompanien/Compagnie

II Bataillon/Battaglione 'Nembo'**

Hauptmann Gerhold/Tenente Romano Ferretto

    5–8 Kompanien/Compagnie

III Bataillon/Battaglione 'Azzurro'

Capitano Alfredo Bussoli/Hauptmann von Nechay

    9–12 Kompanien/Compagnie

13 Kompanie/Compagnia

    Pionier-Zug/Plotone Genio

    Granatwerfer-Zug/Plotone Mortai

    sMG-Zug/Plotone Mitraglieri

14 PaK-Kompanie/Compagnia Controcarri (Never formed)

the survivors were pulled back to Tradate where they rejoined the 'Azzurro' contingent. The regiment was not officially re-formed again until 1 November, subordinated to LXXV Armeekorps, and principally used in anti-partisan activities for which a number of paras were prosecuted after the end of the war. By March 1945 it was fighting in the foothills of the Alps and the few survivors finally surrendered near Aosta on 6 May.

The very last Italian so-called airborne division, 'Azzurra Aquila' (Blue Eagle), formed early in 1945, was really the equivalent of a Luftwaffen-Feld division and only consisted of an Italo-German staff and a motley collection of half-trained Aeronautica Repubblica infantry and anti-aircraft battalions. Postwar, however, a new, elite, Brigata Paracadutisti 'Folgore' was formed that has since been involved in several UN peacekeeping missions, including Afghanistan, Kurdistan and Kosovo.

Unit organization (4):

SS-Fallschirmjäger Bataillon 500/600

The existence of this battalion has caused some confusion down the years, partly over the question of whether it was a penal unit and partly over whether there were one or two battalions. Both questions were actually resolved as long ago as 1985 when former SS-Sturmbannführer (Major) Siegfried Milius, the battalion's last CO, visited a re-enactment group in the United States shortly before his death. The answers to each are both yes and no.

The evolution and history of the Waffen-SS have no place here but in 1937, the year after the creation of the SS-Verfügungstruppe (special disposal troops), the energetic and imaginative CO of the Standarte 'Deutschland', Felix Steiner, proposed the creation of an SS parachute company modelled on the lines of the recently formed air force and army units. At the time, any further expansion of Heinrich Himmler's SS was viewed with intense distrust by the army hierarchy, while Göring was plotting to get all parachute forces incorporated into the Luftwaffe. Thus, despite an abundance of volunteers, Steiner's promising proposal fell on stony official ground and was not resurrected until six years later.

In mid-1943, at the same time as the expansion of the existing Fallschirm-korps, the Führerhauptquartier finally authorized the creation of an SS parachute battalion. It was numbered 500 in keeping with standard German practice for Bewärungs ('probationary') battalions, but this is misleading. Like the 'Dirty Dozen', the men in the real penal battalions were often murderers or rapists who were thrown into suicidal situations with the chance of having their sentences commuted if they survived. The situation was rather different in SS-Fallschirmjäger Bataillon 500. Here, in the first place, less than half the men were convicts, and the recruiting officers were highly selective so those paroled were men sentenced for relatively minor offences such as striking a superior officer, black market activities or being overheard speaking out against the Party or the Führer. Additionally, they regained their former ranks before, not after, proving themselves in battle. Medals and other decorations that may have been stripped from them were also usually restored. Many men had already served out most of their sentences at Dachau or Danzig SS military prisons in any case, while the bulk of the battalion comprised genuine volunteers from throughout the Waffen-SS attracted by a new challenge.

SS-Fallschirmjäger Bataillon 500 began forming at Chlum in Czechoslovakia on 6 September 1943 under SS-Sturmbannführer Herbert Gilhofer, while parachute training was conducted through 3 Fallschirmschule at Kraljevo's Mataruska-Banja airfield in Serbia. (The battalion was highly dependent on the Luftwaffe and until late 1944 wore standard jump smocks with air force chest eagles over their SS field grey and black.) To begin with, the men's newfound talents were wasted and they were solely deployed on foot during February–March 1944 in anti-partisan sweeps in Bosnia, Serbia, Montenegro and Macedonia. That changed in April when the battalion was selected to spearhead a mission to kill, or preferably capture, Marshal Tito at his mountain headquarters, which SS radio intercepts had located outside Drvar in western Bosnia. Codename for the operation was Rößelsprung, and the paras embarked in trucks from Kraljevo to Agram (Zagreb), the Croatian capital, over 21–24 May.

The battalion at this time consisted of 15 officers, 81 NCOs and 896 men, now commanded by SS-Hauptsturmführer (Captain) Kurt Rybka, divided into the Stabskompanie, Nachrichtenzug, 1–3 SS-Fallschirmschützen-Kompanien (each of three Züge) and 4 SS-Fallschirm schwere-Waffen-Kompanie with a platoon each of heavy machine guns, mortars, flamethrowers and anti-tank weapons (Fig. 14, below). Of these, 634 men plus a 20-man team of Luftwaffe communications and intelligence specialists took part in the initial assault. As with Sturmabteilung 'Koch' in 1940, the paras were split into smaller groups with specific objectives, but additionally they had to be ferried in two waves because the assigned Ju 52 wing, II/Transportgeschwader 4, only had 40 operational aircraft. Thirty-four DFS 230B-1s with braking parachutes were also used from 1. and 2./Schleppgruppe 1, and II and III/Luftlande-Lastensegler Geschwader 1, all based around Agram. The towing aircraft comprised 12 Ju 87s and 17 Hs 126s, plus five Czech Avias. Of the men chosen for the mission, 314 participated in the initial parachute assault at 0700hrs on 25 May while 320 were landed in DFS 230s, and 220 from the remainder of the battalion dropped in the second wave at midday.

Operation Rößelsprung was classed as a failure because Tito escaped, although some 6,000 partisans were killed (according to Serb sources, so it was probably higher) and their activities in the region suffered a severe setback. However, Rybka himself had been badly injured by a grenade and when the unwounded men of the battalion remustered at Ljubljana in Slovenia with the few who had not taken part, their strength was down to 292. Now commanded by SS-Hauptsturmführer Siegfried Milius, the depleted SS-Fallschirmjäger Bataillon 500 then fought in Estonia and Lithuania until the beginning of October when the mere 90 survivors were repatriated to Ostmark in Austria.

In the meanwhile a Feldersatz-und-Ausbildungs-Kompanie had been formed and when the two groups were united the battalion lost its probationary status and, renumbered 600, became a genuine all-volunteer unit under the newly promoted SS-Sturmbannführer Milius. It even included Luftwaffe and Kriegsmarine personnel who had transferred to the Waffen-SS. Otto Skorzeny next chose the fittest men from the battalion for Operation Panzerfaust in Budapest. Hitler suspected the Hungarian Regent, Admiral Miklós Horthy, of seeking an armistice with the Soviet Union, and on the morning of 15 October Skorzeny's paras kidnapped Horthy's son Niklaus, forcing him to abdicate.

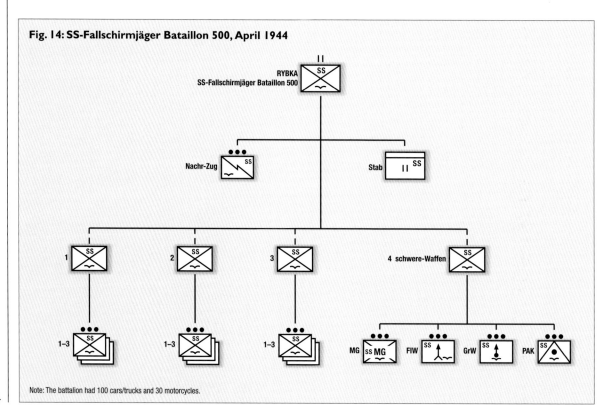

Fig. 14: SS-Fallschirmjäger Bataillon 500, April 1944

Note: The battalion had 100 cars/trucks and 30 motorcycles.

After this, SS-Fallschirmjäger Bataillon 600 spent a month rebuilding at Neustreliz in Mecklenburg, where its strength was brought back to *c*.1,000 men and, on 10 November, it was incorporated into the SS-Jagdverbände. All the battalion's subsequent missions were combined operations under Skorzeny's overall direction. These included Operation Herbstnebel in December when two companies fought as part of SS-Panzerbrigade 150 in the Ardennes. (The only known surviving examples of the SS 1944-pattern jump smock are preserved in the Bastogne historical centre.) After the failure of Hitler's grandiose counteroffensive in the west, Milius's men returned to the Eastern Front as a rearguard for German troops pulling back over the river Oder, but managed to surrender to the Americans rather than the Russians at Hagenau in north Germany at the beginning of May 1945. Unusually for an SS formation that had spent much of its existence on anti-partisan or Commando-style duties, none of the paras were ever convicted of war crimes.

Weapons and equipment

The blitzkrieg campaigns of 1939–41 revealed shortcomings in a wide variety of German equipment, and the war as usual became the mother of invention. Specifically, Göring, Student and others wanted greater firepower for the Fallschirmjäger without adding weight or sacrificing quality. Fortunately, these were also tactical requirements for the regular infantry which, became more urgent after the invasion of Russia when the fact emerged that the Wehrmacht was at last fighting a foe equipped with equal, and in some cases superior, weaponry. Unsurprisingly, huge quantities of captured Soviet infantry equipment, especially sub-machine guns and heavy mortars, were eagerly pressed into German service. What is surprising is that research and development of new armament for the Fallschirmtruppe continued for so long after they had lost their primary role.

In terms of the paras' kit aside from weapons, there were several improvements following combat experience during the blitzkrieg period, as seen already in the section on communications. Proper helmet covers were introduced to supplement the variety of improvised measures in existence. A third-issue jump smock appeared, together with matching trousers in water-pattern camouflage rather than DPM. After the 1943 armistice in Italy, German smocks were also produced in Italian camouflage material and widely worn, especially in 4 Fallschirmjäger Division. SS smocks introduced in 1944 were virtually identical in cut to the Luftwaffe ones, but in pink, brown and green 'polka-dot' camouflage. Lightweight white cotton oversmocks had already been rapidly introduced during the first disastrous winter in Russia, as were warm, quilted jackets and overtrousers; men serving in the Italian mountains also used both. For warmer environments, practical sand-coloured shirts, shorts, jackets and loose-fitting trousers were worn by the Fallschirmjäger from Crete onwards and, although there was never an authorized tropical-pattern jump smock, some may have been tailored privately.

The RZ20 parachutes first used on Crete were also dyed in subdued colours to make it less obvious to the enemy where the paras were deploying once they had landed, but the camouflage was unpopular with the Fallschirmjäger because a myth evolved that the dye was sticky and prevented the 'chutes opening properly! That aside, they were a significant improvement over the RZ16s used in 1940, with a quick-release mechanism and lift webs or 'risers', which help control speed and direction, attached to the harness under the ribs. The containers that carried the paratroops' heavier kit were also modified; originally produced in a range of shapes and sizes, after Crete these were standardized at 150 x 40 x 40cm, each capable of holding 100kg of stores. Another innovation was a cluster of three retro rockets in the nose of the DFS 230C-1 glider for extremely short landings (just 16m, barely more than its own length), without which the mountaintop rescue of Mussolini would have been impossible.

At the most basic level of personal weapons, once the 9mm Walther P38 semi-automatic pistol became virtually standard issue alongside the older existing handguns, the only truly significant development as far as the front-line troops were concerned was the German takeover of Fabrique Nationale in Herstal-lèz-Liège. The Belgian factory manufactured under licence the American 9mm Browning 'Hi-Power', and this was kept in large-scale production for the Wehrmacht as the Pistole 640(b). What every paratrooper in particular appreciated was the fact that the gun had a 13-round magazine instead of the usual eight. During the close encounters the Fallschirmjäger frequently found themselves in, this was a priceless attribute. In the Mediterranean theatre, of course, the ubiquitous 9mm Beretta M34 with seven-round magazine was also frequently seen in German hands. Additionally, the smoothbore Walther Leuchtpistole was fitted with a rifled sleeve, reducing the bore to 22mm but enhancing range and accuracy, especially when firing parachute flares; in this guise it was renamed Kampfpistole, while the final version, designated Sturmpistole, could also fire rifle grenades.

Going up the scale, the 9mm Beretta M38/42 sub-machine gun (smg) was used by practically all the former 'Folgore' and 'Nembo' volunteers in 4 Fallschirmjäger Division, and widely throughout the Wehrmacht in Italy as well. It was fed by a 20- or 40-round box magazine and had a cyclic rate of fire of 550rpm. Ammunition for Italian weapons remained readily available even after the armistice because most industry was concentrated in the German-occupied north of the country. This was fortunate because the Italian 9mm 'short' round was lower powered than the German Parabellum so, although Italian ammunition could be fired safely from German weapons, the reverse was positively dangerous. Other than the Beretta, the 9mm Erma MP40 remained standard Fallschirmjäger issue; the MP40/II introduced in 1943, which held two magazines side by side, was not a success.

The same was true of the 7.92mm Walther Gew41, the German army's first serious attempt to produce a semi-automatic self-loading rifle (SLR). The Americans had actually been first in the field here, with John Garand's .30in. M1 that became the US Army's standard rifle from 1936. Although rather heavy, it had a useful eight-round clip magazine. The Gew41 had a 10-round box magazine, but this had to be reloaded by hand rather than simply replaced, just like that on the 6.5mm Breda M30 light machine gun (lmg) – a slow process in the middle of a firefight. In addition, the rather primitive gas-operated mechanism made the Gew41 very muzzle-heavy and difficult to aim accurately other than with an elbow rest. Its later derivative, the Gew43, had an improved mechanism, a detachable box magazine and was much lighter, but was almost exclusively used by snipers because by this time German assault rifles had made their battlefield debut.

Once again, it was the Americans who really pioneered this concept with John Browning's .30in. M1918 automatic rifle. He designed it with the intention of giving infantry a portable weapon with which they could provide their own suppressive fire when charging across no man's land. Like the British Bren, though, the BAR was really an lmg in all but name since it was too long and heavy to aim and fire from the shoulder. Nevertheless, it soldiered on as a squad support weapon until the introduction of the Armalite after the Korean War.

In 1939–41 German infantry had nothing comparable to the American weapons they were soon to encounter in Tunisia and Italy, because the Treaty of Versailles had so hampered prewar R&D. Poor rate of fire was thus the principal criticism of the otherwise sturdy, reliable and accurate bolt-action rifles in service during the blitzkrieg years. These were still satisfactory for positional battles when combined with machine guns, but not really for mobile warfare. Moreover, the campaign in the west showed that there was rarely need for the long-range capability of a conventional rifle, meaning that barrels could be shorter (enhancing rate of fire) and cartridges less powerful (reducing recoil and user fatigue, thereby improving accuracy).

Even before the war, the German Polte firm had been experimenting with cartridge lengths and weights and produced an intermediate 7.92mm (.32in.) round more powerful than that in a handgun but less than in a rifle. With the conclusion of the French campaign, two other firms – Haenel and Walther – tendered for an OKW contract to produce a 'machine carbine' (Maschinen-karabiner) using this cartridge. The idea, fairly obviously, was to combine the single-shot accuracy of a standard rifle at 400–500m range with the rapid-fire attributes of an lmg, but without the disadvantages of an smg. With the benefit of two decades of technological improvement, the Germans were more successful than Browning. Each firm adopted a similar approach, with what has become the familiar straight-line layout. Both the MKb42(H) and (W) were gas operated with an open/locked piston/bolt mechanism for automatic or single-shot operation, and had 30-round curved box magazines. (The cartridges were rimmed so a long straight-edged magazine was impractical.) When tested in combat during the winter of 1942–43, the Haenel design proved superior and was put into large-scale production, inaccurately designated MP43. This was later changed to StG44, or Sturmgewehr 44; unbelievably for something so trivial, the weapon's name itself caused political infighting with Hitler running his usual interference!

Although the Luftwaffe expressed keen interest in the MKb project to begin with, and the paras did later use the StG44 in significant quantities, the assessors were not impressed with the 640m/sec muzzle velocity conferred by the relatively low-powered cartridge coupled to a short 36.4cm barrel. The search continued for something more suited to the paratroops' anticipated needs and the RLM asked six firms to design a similar weapon using a full-power 'long' 7.92mm cartridge, accepting the fact that this also necessitated a longer barrel (50.8cm) to prevent excessive recoil as had earlier been the case with the extemporized Gew33/40(t). Of the six designs, the one submitted by Rheinmetall-Borsig was chosen but put into production by Krieghof because the parent firm was already inundated with existing work.

The FG42 (Fallschirmgewehr 42) in its original guise was unquestionably one of the most aesthetically pleasing rifles of the war, although it suffered from trying to incorporate too many features in one 'universal' weapon. Everything possible was done to save weight, including an ergonomically

Dress standards inevitably deteriorated on campaign, as this MG42 section admirably demonstrates. The weapon actually has a drum magazine fitted, but the men are all carrying loose 50-round belts or boxes of 7.92mm ammunition, and have netting loosely covering their helmets into which to tuck foliage.

designed, stamped-steel shoulder stock, a bipod that proved rather flimsy for sustained use, and a hinged bayonet resembling an ice pick. The pistol grip was angled backwards for greater comfort. Where to position the magazine took much discussion. If the receiver was beneath the barrel, as on the MKb42 series, it would make the gun difficult to operate as an lmg. If it was above, as on the British Bren, the gunner would be partially unsighted. Taking a leaf from the Italian book, Rheinmetall eventually opted for a side-loading 20-round magazine. The design of any tool demands compromise, but in eliminating some drawbacks on the FG42, Rheinmetall introduced two new ones. The torque effect from the side magazine mounting coupled to the lightweight bipod made the gun swivel from its target when used as an lmg, while the magazine tended to catch on loose clothing when it was carried as an assault rifle. Nevertheless, Kesselring amongst many others was highly impressed and the FG42 was put into production purely for the Fallschirmjäger.

Sadly, by the time this happened in 1943, the paras' role had been so truncated that the weapon's manufacture was also cut short, despite economies such as a simple wooden stock and conventional pistol grip. Only about 7,000 of both versions were ultimately produced. The rifle made its combat debut at Gran Sasso and those men lucky enough to receive one jealously preserved it. The FG42 actually had a higher rate of fire than the army weapon despite its barrel length (c.750rpm cyclic compared to 500) and an obviously higher muzzle velocity (c.760m/sec compared to 640), the latter attribute conferred greater stopping power as well as range. There was no real equivalent amongst the Western Allies, perhaps the closest being the .30in. Winchester M1A1 developed specifically for airborne troops from the M1 carbine, with a folding stock, pistol grip and 15- or 30-round box magazine.

Stopping power was perhaps also the greatest attribute of the 7.92mm Mauser MG42, which very few people would dispute was the finest machine gun of the entire war. The MG34 with which the Wehrmacht began its campaigns was already a superior weapon, but because of its very quality was expensive and time consuming to manufacture. The Wehrmacht's need after the beginning of the Russian campaign was for rapid production of all types of weapon even if it necessitated lowering standards, but Mauser remarkably succeeded in achieving the former without really resorting to the latter. Benefiting from lessons already taught in the earlier transformation of the MP38 smg into the MP40, the firm reduced the number of precisely machined components and introduced more pressed and stamped parts that could be produced and assembled both cheaply and quickly. Mauser also took the opportunity to improve the belt feed and the quick barrel-change mechanisms, making it much smoother and faster in operation. This resulted in a drastic increase in rate of fire from the MG34's already formidable 800–900rpm to an unheard of 1,200rpm. It did not take the Wehrmacht's opponents long to distinguish the characteristic 'ripping' sound of an MG42 from the steadier beat of other machine guns, and the weapon became a very effective psychological as well as physical deterrent to resistance in either the attack or defence. The only drawback to the rate of fire was a sharp decrease in accuracy except when mounted on the sustained fire tripod, but this was rarely a tactical disadvantage. Additionally, the MG42 was less prone to jam through dust and dirt than the predecessor it never completely supplanted. None of the Germans' adversaries ever developed anything remotely competitive and 50 years later the British armed forces were still waiting for one.

Returning to the first paragraph of this section, one of the Soviet weapons that most impressed the German infantry in 1941 was a 120mm mortar firing a bomb roughly four times the weight of that of their own standard 8.1cm GrW34, and to more than twice the range. Captured examples plus huge stocks of ammunition were enthusiastically turned against their former owners and a German copy was rushed into production as the sGrW42. By definition, a mortar fires at an elevation of more than 45 degrees, making such a heavy weapon almost comparable in effectiveness to a howitzer – but going back to a familiar theme, howitzers are time consuming and very expensive to manufacture as well as needing a tractor to tow them, and these were three luxuries the Wehrmacht was rapidly finding it could not afford. The sGrW42 thus filled a hitherto unforeseen gap in the German arsenal and entire heavy mortar companies and battalions became commonplace, not least amongst the Fallschirmjäger divisions. At 282kg the weapon weighed five times as much as a GrW34 but could still be manhandled at need, although it was generally employed in a static role. It fired a 15.79kg bomb to a range of 5,940m. A second mortar introduced especially for airborne operations was a cut-down version of the 8.1cm GrW34, designated GrW42 kurz, but it was not a success due to diminished range and accuracy.

Apart from the sGrW42, another weapon widely used by the Fallschirmtruppe that also packed a massive punch while being simple to manufacture and sufficiently light in weight to be manhandled, towed behind a Ketten-Krad, or even dropped by parachute, was the Nebelwerfer. The word literally means 'fog thrower' but in military terminology 'smoke discharger', both of which are almost as misleading as the British use of 'tank' in World War I. Cutting a fascinating story short, while the Treaty of Versailles limited German developments in conventional artillery, it said nothing about rockets (just as it ignored gliders). Taking advantage of this loophole, the pre-Nazi Reichsheer set up an R&D facility at the Kummersdorf artillery proving ground under Walter Dornberger – later Wernher von Braun's boss on the A4/V2 project. The army at the time (c.1930) was already looking for improved ways of laying smokescreens, so the Inter-Allied Control Commission was easily hoodwinked by the double entendre of 'Nebelwerfer'!

By the summer of 1941 the Fallschirmjäger had already field tested a handful of Dornberger's prototypes on Crete so were receptive to the idea of an air-portable weapon that could deliver a more substantial barrage than their existing artillery. Alongside the 7.5 and 10.5cm lG40 recoilless guns, the 15cm WGr41 Nebelwerfer thus became one of the most significant weapons in their armoury during 1942–45. It was first used in the early stages of the Russian campaign when it encountered rival opposition from the Soviet Katyusha multiple-launch rocket system, and in small quantities in North Africa where the Allies at the time had nothing comparable. The Nebelwerfer employed a launch system little more sophisticated than you would use in a domestic firework display, although ignition was electrical rather than by blue touch paper! A cluster of six light steel tubes was mounted on the split-trail carriage of an obsolete 3.7cm PaK35/36; the Wurfgranate 41 Spreng rockets were inserted from the rear and the ignition circuit sent them off at two-second intervals towards a target up to 7km distant. Needless to say, 'stand well clear' was no idle warning for the four-man crews, 15m being the recommended distance, but the men were used to this because their recoilless guns were almost as dangerous.

The rockets were highly unusual. Dornberger saw that a principal problem with conventional designs was that the imbalance created by putting the warhead in front, or on top, of the solid fuel motor caused wobbling and even toppling in flight, making 'accuracy' meaningless. He therefore placed the motor foremost, further improving stability by making it exhaust through 14 angled venturis that imparted spin. Although this system was abandoned on later, larger, artillery rockets due to complexity and cost, the 'Moaning Minnie' was rightly respected and feared by the Allies because a salvo of six projectiles with 10kg warheads landing close to one spot caused vast destruction. The only disadvantage the Germans soon discovered was that the Nebelwerfer sites were impossible to conceal and brought swift retribution unless the launchers could be relocated very quickly after firing. Recoilless guns had a similar drawback, of course, despite which Rheinmetall continued development with the 10.5cm lG42 and '43 that each fired the same ammunition as the army's standard leFH18 howitzer to a range of c.3,400m. Both weapons could be broken down into four or more loads for parachute drops. In Italy, however, they were never deployed in this fashion and for tactical reasons the Fallschirmjäger continued to use the 7.5cm GebG36 mountain gun once the problem of firing on a flat trajectory that had so plagued the weapon in 1940 was understood.

Rockets were also used later as infantry-portable anti-tank weapons after the Germans encountered the American 'bazooka' in Tunisia, but long before this the Fallschirmtruppe had been insistently demanding a parachute-droppable gun more effective than the old PaK 35/36 and smaller and lighter than the 5cm PaK 38. The 2.8cm sPzB41 met all these needs admirably at ranges up to circa 500m, being able to penetrate armour sloped at 30 degrees more than 50mm thick. This remarkable achievement was accomplished by using the squeeze bore principle devised by Hermann Gerlich in the 1920s. (British artillery 'experts' were still saying it was impossible with existing technology until an example of the German gun was captured in North Africa in late summer 1941.)

The barrel was tapered from 2.8cm at the breech to 2cm at the muzzle, the former being the calibre of the propellant cartridge and the latter of the dense tungsten-cored projectile. This was encased in a soft, flanged lead sheath that compressed as it travelled through the barrel, resulting in the incredible muzzle velocity of 1,400m/sec – greater than that of the 7.5cm PaK 40. A muzzle brake was fitted to absorb some of the enormous recoil. The standard gun had a conventional two-wheel split-trail carriage but the airborne version had a single tubular steel pole on which the gunner sat in between two ex-fighter aircraft tailwheels. There was a small splinter shield but no elevation or traverse mechanism, aiming being over open sights with the magnesium tip on the round showing clearly where it had struck.

Rome, 10 September 1943. A group of Fallschirmjäger enters the Eternal City under cover of a 42mm PaK 41. A rare weapon based on the PaK 37 mount, it was produced in limited quantities during 1942. First employed in North Africa, it was also used to equip Fallschirmjäger units. (Archivio Ufficio Storico Stato Maggiore Esercito (AUSSME) – via Filippo Cappellano)

Although it was a remarkably effective weapon for its size, the sPzB41 and its larger stablemate, the 4.2cm PJK41 that saw service with the Ramcke Brigade, were fated like many other promising German designs to be abandoned when supplies of tungsten and manganese became scarce. By this time, however, the Wehrmacht had come to realize the advantages of low-velocity hollow-charge anti-tank weapons that were simple and cheap enough to produce in hundreds of thousands. The Panzerfaust and Panzerschreck needed little instruction to use and essentially brought an effective short-range anti-tank capability within reach of every infantryman. Like the sPzB41, both are discussed and illustrated in colour in Osprey's Warrior 38: *Fallschirmjäger* by the same author, but one variant of the Panzerschreck deserves special mention here: the Püppchen. This utilized virtually the same lightweight carriage as the airborne version of the sPzP41 but with a modified Panzerschreck, or 8.8cm Racketenpanzerbüchse 54, in place of the gun barrel. There were two problems with bazooka-style weapons: very limited range (*c.*100m) and the fact that the rocket exhaust instantly identified from where it had been fired. The Püppchen, or Racketenwerfer 43, had a closed breech so the exhaust from the rocket was enclosed until it left the muzzle; this also imparted greater velocity so the weapon was moderately accurate out to 700m. The 88mm-diameter warhead could easily penetrate 100mm of armour plate, enough to destroy or cripple any American or British tank. Like many late-war developments, however, the Püppchen was only produced in relatively small quantities.

Apart from the items already singled out, the Fallschirmtruppe in the Mediterranean theatre of operations used standard Wehrmacht equipment including conventional artillery, anti-tank, anti-aircraft and assault guns, about which many other books are available.

Tactics

Although Crete marked the end of German large-scale airborne operations, it did not mark the end of the development of Fallschirmjäger's airborne tactics. Although lessons learned were put into practice only in a limited scale, they were learnt nevertheless. Not by chance, after Crete new transport planes, gliders, weapons and new parachutes were developed; jump discipline was enhanced and training was improved. For the planned attack against Malta some night jump training took place, although the final plan only included daylight jumps. Also, for the first time since Eben Emael, paratroopers and troop-carrier units were trained together. Fallschirmjäger began to practise jumping with weapons attached, thus filling a notable gap in their techniques. Moreover, their training now enabled them to be either airdropped or glider-borne, thus making good for the losses suffered by the Sturm-Regiment.

Still, in 1942 Fallschirmjäger were intended to play a strategic role in the planned invasion of Malta, and in Tunisia and in Sicily actually played a major role as a kind of rapid deployment force. The deterioration in quantity and quality of German airborne units only reached a critical point in late 1944. In the summer of that year, Student could still reckon on some 30,000 jump-trained Fallschirmjäger, mostly in 1 (whose personnel was 50 per cent jump trained) and in 2 (with some 30 per cent jump-trained personnel) Fallschirmjäger Divisions. Yet, by this date, Allied air supremacy and Germany's loss of initiative had already put an end to large-scale airborne operations.

There were many reasons why Germany lacked the ability to make adequate use of her airborne forces, but two major ones. Firstly, Germany simply lacked an adequate number of transport planes to implement a major airdrop. Secondly, since Crete had shown that the Fallschirmjäger no longer possessed strategic surprise; local, tactical surprise was a basic pre-requisite for success, which required strict operational secrecy. Since Hitler was firmly (and probably rightly) convinced that Italians could not assure secrecy, there is little wonder that he was anything but inclined toward Operation Herkules.

The planned invasion of Malta was not only the last, missed, opportunity for the Fallschirmäger to play a strategic role, but the cancellation of the operation limited the implementation of new weapons and equipment, as well as of the new, improved, techniques and tactics. Go 242 gliders were used in Sicily (just to fall victim to air raids), the FG42 gun was used at Gran Sasso (during which not a single shot was fired) and on this occasion, as in the raid on Leros, gliders carried the Fallschirmjäger.

Yet, by this date, Fallschirmjäger had already proved valuable as a sort of elite infantry, a role that characterized their fighting experiences in the Mediterranean theatre of operations. Many explanations had been given for it, but their effectiveness in defence was also a direct consequence of their tactical training. Since their main role was the seizure of key objectives, which had to be held until relieved by land units, Fallschirmjäger were trained to stand at all costs and, according to the German tactical doctrine, to counter-attack where necessary to maintain their positions. Although these tactics were to prove costly, they also ensured that Fallschirmjäger-held positions were always the hardest to overcome.

El Alamein, October 1942

On 23 October 1942 Italian X Corps held the southern portion of the Axis front at El Alamein with three divisions in the front line: 27 Infantry 'Brescia', 185 Parachute 'Folgore' and 17 Infantry 'Pavia'. Between the 'Brescia' and 'Folgore'

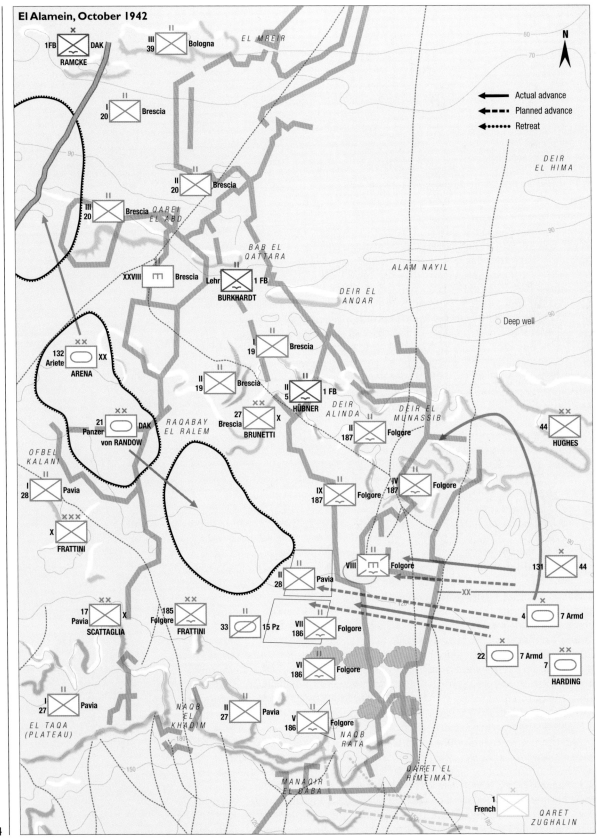

El Alamein, October 1942

Actual advance
Planned advance
Retreat

N

EL MREIR

DEIR EL HIMA

QAREI EL ABD

BAB EL QATTARA

ALAM NAYIL

DEIR EL ANQAR

Deep well

DEIR ALINDA

DEIR EL MUNASSIB

RAQABAY EL RALEM

OFBEL KALANI

NAQB EL KHADIM

NAQB RATA

EL TAQA (PLATEAU)

MANAQIR EL BABA

QARET EL HIMEIMAT

QARET ZUGHALIN

1FB DAK
RAMCKE

III 39 Bologna

I 20 Brescia

II 20 Brescia

III 20 Brescia

XXVIII Brescia

Lehr 1 FB
BURKHARDT

132 Ariete
ARENA

I 19 Brescia

II 19 Brescia

II 5 1 FB
HÜBNER

27 Brescia
BRUNETTI

II 187 Folgore

44 HUGHES

21 Panzer DAK
von RANDOW

IX 187 Folgore

IV 187 Folgore

I 28 Pavia

X FRATTINI

VIII Folgore

131 44

I 28 Pavia

4 7 Armd

17 Pavia X
SCATTAGLIA

185 Folgore
FRATTINI

33 15 Pz

VII 186 Folgore

22 7 Armd

7 HARDING

VI 186 Folgore

I 27 Pavia

II 27 Pavia

V 186 Folgore

1 French

Captain Costantino Ruspoli, who died on 26 October 1942 at El Alamein earning a Military Gold Medal, Italy's highest decoration. Member of a noble family, he was born in New York in 1891. He volunteered for the army in 1940 and joined the paratroopers in 1941. His brother Marescotti was the commander of the 'Ruspoli Group'. (Archivio Ufficio Storico Stato Maggiore Esercito (AUSSME) – via Filippo Cappellano)

divisions were two battalions of Ramcke's 1 Fallschirmjäger Brigade (Hübner and Burkhardt), while two other were stationed to the north, in the area between Italian X and XX Corps. In reserve, in X Corps area, were the 132 'Ariete' armoured divisions and the German 21 Panzer Division.

Opposite them was the British XIII Corps, whose task in Operation Lightfoot was to breach the Axis main line of resistance and engage the two armoured divisions, thus preventing them from being switched to the north where the main thrust of Lightfoot was to take place. Although inferior both in numbers and weapons, the Italian Paracadutisti and the Fallschirmjäger successfully prevented the enemy breakthrough.

On the night of 24 October, the British 22nd Brigade (supported by 7th Queen's Royal of 131st Brigade) and 1 Free French Brigade attacked the Italian positions north and west of Qaret el Himeimat, which were held by 186 Reggimento Paracadutisti. Unexpectedly, the Italians promptly reacted with their artillery, while the Paracadutisti held their positions and launched counter-attacks using small raiding parties, which approached enemy positions under cover and showered them with hand-grenades. At first light the Free

Lieutenant General Enrico Frattini, the first commander of the 'Folgore' Division, here portrayed in Egypt in August 1942. While commanding the Army's Engineer School, in 1941 (aged 50) he volunteered for the paratroopers and, after achieving jump brevet, he became divisional commander. He was captured at El Alamein. (Archivio Ufficio Storico Stato Maggiore Esercito (AUSSME) – via Filippo Cappellano)

French Brigade – now attacked by the German 33 Aufklärungs-Abteilung – were compelled to withdraw, while 22nd Brigade only succeeded in breaching the first line of defence, though they successfully repulsed a counter-attack by the Italian 28th Infantry Regiment.

Again, on the night of the 25th, the 131st and 22nd Brigades tried to breach the Italian main line of resistance, which they only partially succeeded in doing. At daybreak elements of 'Ariete' and 21 Panzer closed the breach, thus causing General Horrocks to change his plan: 4th (Light) Brigade was to attack the Italian positions at Deir el Munassib trying to outflank them. The attack started on the evening of 25 October, and hit the positions of 187 Reggimento Paracadutisti, which, like the 186th, proved a hard nut to crack. Forward defences were crushed but, once more, the Italians reacted forcefully and on the 26th the British attack lost its impetus.

XIII Corps had failed to attain its objective, although it successfully prevented the two armoured divisions from being redeployed northwards. For a week the battle focused to the north, until on 3 November the Italian X Corps was ordered to withdraw. Lacking motor transport and supplies, many Italian divisions – the 'Folgore' amongst them – simply dissolved while retreating. On the contrary, partly thanks to a captured British supply column, many Fallschirmjäger of the Ramcke Brigade succeeded in making it. The most notable victim was Burkhardt's Lehr-Bataillon, which was captured near Fuka by British troops. At the end of November Ramcke handed over command to Oberstleutnant Kroh, and two months later what was left of the brigade was in Tunisia.

Primosole Bridge, July 1943

For the British paratroopers, Primosole Bridge foreshadowed the disaster at Arnhem. For the Fallschirmjäger, it was a perfect example of what the capability to react, swiftness, boldness and good luck could accomplish. The bridge was a key objective in Montgomery's race to Messina; the plan (codenamed Fustian) was to seize it using elements of 1st Parachute Division, which were to be relieved by 50th Infantry Division advancing from the south across the Malati Bridge, which was to be seized by Commandos. As soon as 50th Division crossed the Simeto River, the city of Catania would have been close at hand.

Lathbury's 1st Parachute Brigade suffered ill luck from the very start of the operation. Immediately after take-off on the night of 13 July 1943, their transports were attacked twice by friendly anti-aircraft fire, 14 were shot down and many others turned back or simply scattered. Only 12 officers and 283 other ranks, out of 1,856 intended, landed at Primosole in the first hours of 14 July, immediately moving to their targets. Frost's 2nd Battalion took over Italian positions in a hill south of the bridge, renamed 'Johnny I', while Pearson's 1st and Yeldham's 3rd Battalions took over the bridge.

Apparently, British paratroopers were facing no resistance; Italian soldiers began to surrender en masse, abandoning their positions and their weapons. But the Fallschirmjäger held firm. Some hours before British paratroopers were dropped, Schmidt's 1 Fallschirm-MG Bataillon had established positions south of the bridge, close to the 'Johnny III' position. Soon after the British landing it began to fire at enemy positions on 'Johnny I', causing great concern amongst Frost's men. North of the bridge Hauptmann Franz Stangenberg, a staff officer of 1 Fallschirmjäger Division, soon realized what was going on and reacted swiftly. He gathered every man available and, along with Hauptmann Erich Fassl's Nachrichten Kompanie, attacked the British positions close to the bridge.

Although numerically inferior, Stangenberg and Fassl could rely on greater firepower thanks to the nearby Flak Batterie. Also, Schmidt's MG Bataillon attack against the British positions at 'Johnny I' provoked further confusion. Faulty radios and lack of ammunition prevented the British paratroopers from arranging a better defence and, at dusk, Lathbury decided to abandon the northern end of the bridge. At 1830hrs, one hour after their withdrawal from the bridge, Lathbury ordered his men to withdraw to 'Johnny II', thus abandoning even the southern end of the bridge. One hour later, the vanguard of 4th Armoured Brigade established contact with the 2nd Battalion, while Schmidt's MG Bataillon retreated north across the bridge. That very night, Lathbury's men were evacuated.

Meanwhile, other German units had arrived to help Stangenberg and Fassl, most notably Hauptmann Paul Adolf's Fallschirm-Pioniere Bataillon 1 and an advanced party of I/FJR 4. A defence line was established north of the Simeto River, while 1 and 3 Fallschirm-Pioniere Kompanie established a bridgehead to the south. On the morning of 15 July they faced the first of a series of attacks, this time led by the 9th Durham Light Infantry supported by 44th RTR. British troops succeeded in crossing the bridge, but the German anti-tank guns destroyed three Shermans and fire from the Fallschirmjäger positions forced 9th DLI to retreat. Only by chance a portion of the southern end of the bridge was secured, because the commander of 1 Fallschirm-Pioniere Kompanie misunderstood an order and withdrew north of it.

A new British attempt was made on the 16th across a ford by 8th DLI, which succeeded in establishing a bridgehead with two companies, although they suffered heavy losses. The defending Fallschirmjäger took full advantage of the terrain, characterized by many large vineyards and olive trees, and also by a sunken road running north-west of the bridge that enabled concealed movements. However, they too suffered severe losses, and had to finally

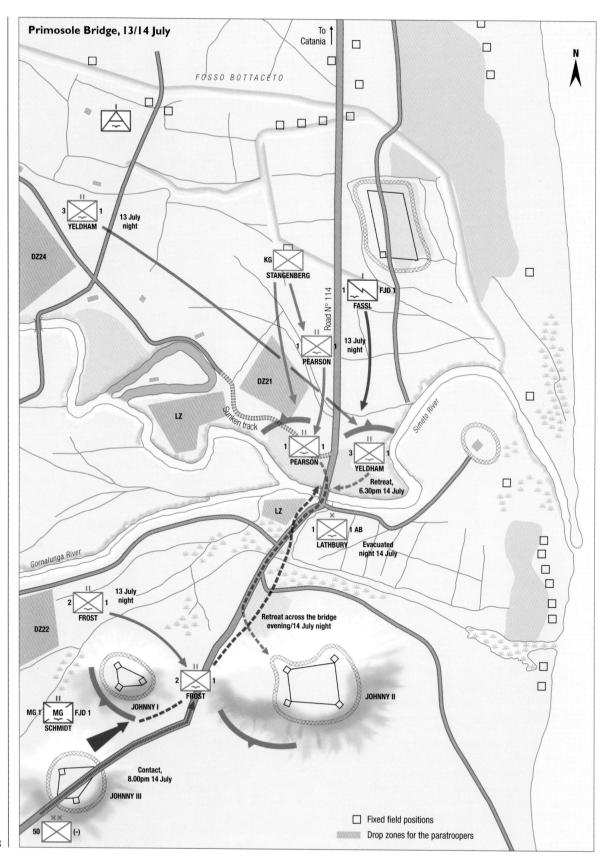

Primosole Bridge, 13/14 July

To Catania

N

FOSSO BOTTACETO

3 | YELDHAM | 1
13 July night

DZ24

KG STANGENBERG

1 FJD 1 FASSL

1 PEARSON
Road Nº 114
13 July night

DZ21

Sunken track

LZ

1 PEARSON 1

3 YELDHAM 1

Simeto River

Retreat, 6.30pm 14 July

LZ

1 LATHBURY 1 AB
Evacuated night 14 July

Gornalunga River

2 FROST 1
13 July night

DZ22

Retreat across the bridge evening/14 July night

2 FROST 1

JOHNNY II

MG 1 MG FJD 1 SCHMIDT

JOHNNY I

JOHNNY II

Contact, 8.00pm 14 July

JOHNNY III

50 (-)

☐ Fixed field positions

▨ Drop zones for the paratroopers

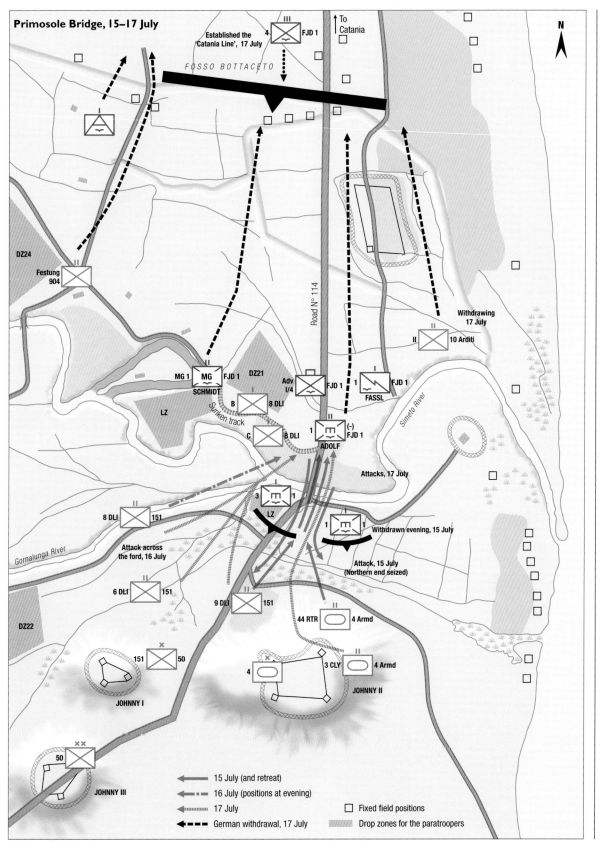

Primosole Bridge, 15–17 July

Established the 'Catania Line', 17 July

III 4 FJD 1

To Catania

FOSSO BOTTACETO

N

DZ24
Festung 904

Road N° 114

Withdrawing 17 July

II 10 Arditi

MG 1 | MG SCHMIDT | FJD 1
DZ21

Adv I/4 | FJD 1

1 | FJD 1 | FASSL

Sunken track

B | 8 DLI

LZ

C | 8 DLI

II 1 | ADOLF | (-) FJD 1

Simeto River

Attacks, 17 July

3 | 1 | LZ

1 | 1 | Withdrawn evening, 15 July

8 DLI | 151

Gornalunga River

Attack across the ford, 16 July

Attack, 15 July (Northern end seized)

6 DLI | 151

DZ22

9 DLI | 151

44 RTR | 4 Armd

151 | 50

4

3 CLY | 4 Armd

JOHNNY II

JOHNNY I

50

JOHNNY III

15 July (and retreat)

16 July (positions at evening)

17 July

German withdrawal, 17 July

☐ Fixed field positions

▨ Drop zones for the paratroopers

79

withdraw due to the loss of all their anti-tank weapons. A further British attack on the 17th, led by the 6th, 8th, 9th DLI and the 3rd County of London Yeomanry ('Sharpshooters') finally succeeded.

No longer capable of stopping enemy armour, the Germans withdrew north to the Bottaceto Ditch. Hauptmann Adolf did attempt to destroy the bridge using a lorry loaded with two aircraft bombs, but he was wounded and died the following day. Hauptmann Fassl and what was left of his Nachrichten Kompanie, in all 17 men, surrendered. However, the seizure of Primosole Bridge did not prove to be the breakthrough the Allies sought after, as on the 17th FJR 4 had established a defence line on the Bottaceto Ditch that would hold out until 5 August. The 'Grün Teufel' had shown what they could do.

Mussolini's rescue from Gran Sasso, September 1943

Although this is one of the Fallschirmjäger's most typical 'Commando'-style actions, thanks to Goebbels' propaganda it is much more famous as a Waffen-SS raid. After he had been arrested on 26 July 1943, the Italian dictator Benito Mussolini was brought first to the island of Ponza, and then to a hotel on the Gran Sasso massif in the central Apennines. A special SS intelligence team formed by the Sicherheitsdienst and led by SS-Sturmbannführer Herbert Kappler and SS-Hauptsturmführer Otto Skorzeny, helped by Hauptmann Langguth, XI Fliegerkorps' intelligence officer, managed to pinpoint his location and a rescue operation was put into action. On 11 September Student summoned Major Harald Mors, commander of I/FJR 7, and Skorzeny to inform them of his decision and the date for the operation was set for the following day.

The 'Duce' was held in the Hotel Campo Imperatore (Emperor's Camp), situated on a 2,100m-high plateau dominated by the peak of Gran Sasso. The hotel could only be accessed via a cableway. Details of the position were scarce

11 September 1943, Mussolini is escorted from the Hotel Campo Imperatore by the Fallschirmjäger who rescued him. First from right, standing, is Major Mors; second from right is Oberleutnant Schulze, CO of 3 Kompanie, which seized the lower cable station. (Archivio Ufficio Storico Stato Maggiore Esercito (AUSSME) – via Filippo Cappellano)

and low-level reconnaissance was impossible, as this would have alerted Mussolini's guards. The only solution was a coup de main assault relying on good luck and timing, and this was exactly the plan that Mors put together. He selected Oberleutnant Georg von Berlepsch's 1 Fallschirmjäger Kompanie to land on the plateau using DFS 230 assault gliders, while 2 and 3 Kompanie and the battalion HQ were to seize the lower cableway station.

At 0300hrs on 12 September a motorized column composed of the battalion HQ, 2 and 3 Fallschirmjäger Kompanie started its c.60km march to L'Aquila and from there to the town of Assergi, close to Gran Sasso. At 1400hrs, while the bulk of the column reached Assergi, an advance party under the command of Oberleutnant Weber seized the lower cableway station, disarming the Italian guards without any problems. One hour earlier, at 1305hrs, the first group of three gliders took off from the airport at Pratica di Mare, soon followed by the rest. Because of low clouds they could not reach the projected altitude, but less than one hour later – at 1403hrs – the first glider was released 3km from the target, soon followed by the others.

The action itself was over in a matter of moments. The gliders approached silently and unseen, and the Fallschirmjäger's presence was not noticed until after they had landed. Some of the Italian guards, in all about 100 Carabinieri (military police), belatedly attempted to put up some kind of resistance at the entrance to the hotel, but they were soon overwhelmed by a group of Fallschirmjäger who had landed less than 40m from the entrance. Only one of the gliders crash landed causing three injuries, the only casualties from the operation. Immediately, a Carabinieri officer began to order his men to cease firing, while a group of Fallschirmjäger led by an Italian-speaking officer located Mussolini. It was all over in less than ten minutes.

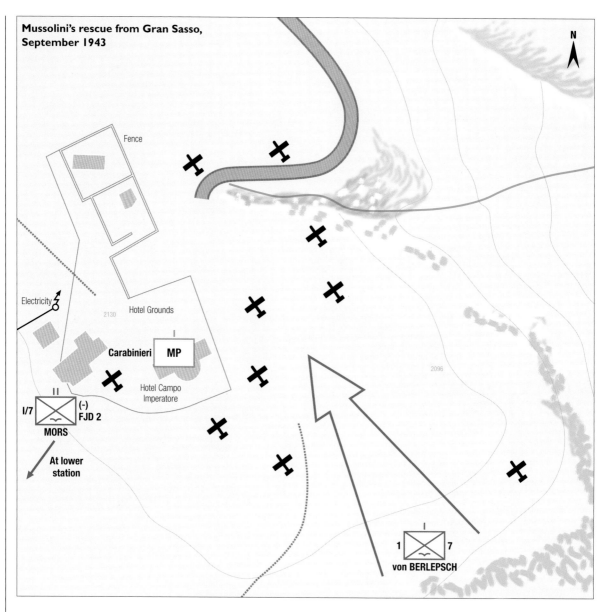

Mussolini's rescue from Gran Sasso, September 1943

N

Fence

Electricity

2130

Hotel Grounds

Carabinieri MP

Hotel Campo
Imperatore

I/7 (-) FJD 2
MORS

At lower
station

2096

1 7
von BERLEPSCH

Fallschirmjäger bidding farewell to a
Fieseler Storch as it takes off from
the Gran Sasso plateau with
Mussolini and Otto Skorzeny on
board. (Count E.G. Vitetti collection)

ABOVE A series of photographs taken at Preatica di Mare shortly before I Kompanie, FJR 7, took off for the Gran Sasso. These were later published in *Signal* magazine. Fallschirmjäger preparing before take-off on the morning of 12 September 1943. (Count E.G. Vitetti collection)

An air-raid alarm compelled them to seek cover for a short period. (Count E.G. Vitetti collection)

While the Carabinieri were disarmed, Mors reached the hotel using the cableway and met von Berlepsch and his 110 Fallschirmjäger. Minutes later a Fieseler Fi 156 'Storch' piloted by Student's pilot, Hauptmann Gerlach, landed on the plateau to take the 'Duce' to safety. At this point Skorzeny, who had arrived in one of the gliders, insisted that he should accompany Mussolini. At about 1540hrs the Fieseler landed at Pratica di Mare, where Mussolini – still accompanied by Skorzeny – was taken aboard a Ju 52 that flew him to Germany. Skorzeny boasted that he was the one who led the action, something Goebbels' propaganda kept repeating in the following days; to Student's great dismay the role of the Fallschirmjäger was not mentioned.

Anzio, February 1944

Although Fallschirmjäger units displayed great skill and endurance in several defensive battles during the Italian campaign, their performances during the German counteroffensives at Anzio on 16–20 February and 27 February–3 March clearly shows how they were unfit for offensive action in this theatre. A first, basic reason for this failure was their lack of heavy weapons; although a 1944 Fallschirmjäger Division bore little resemblance to the organization of 7 Flieger Division in 1941, it did remain, however, a lightly armed unit. A Fallschirm-Regiment only had one heavy machine gun for every 134 men, and a mortar or a 75mm infantry gun for every 59 men; in comparison, a Panzergrenadier Regiment had a heavy machine gun for every 88 men and a mortar or a self-propelled infantry gun (either 75 and 105mm) for every 57 men. The average 1944 Infanterie Regiment had a heavy machine gun for every 116 men and a mortar or 75mm infantry gun for every 58 men.

Moreover, Fallschirmjäger divisions lacked heavy artillery (most notably 4 FJD, which was left with no artillery at all) and any kind of armoured vehicles, although its Panzer-Abwehr and Flak units were well equipped. But their greatest drawback was the dramatic expansion of the Fallschirm-Korps between late 1943 and 1944. In a period of around six months the number of Fallschirmjäger divisions was increased from two to six, mainly using cadres and entire units drawn from 1 and 2 Fallschirmjäger Divisions. The ranks of these new divisions were filled with new recruits and Luftwaffe service personnel, in many cases lacking even basic infantry training. When the divisions had enough time to train their new recruits they could operate well, but, as was the case with 4 Fallschirmjäger Division, when the division was thrown into the battle lacking both training and weapons, the inevitable result was a poor performance coupled with heavy losses.

On 16 February 1944 14 Armee launched a major counteroffensive against the Allied beachhead at Anzio with the aim of wiping it out. A first wave of infantry and Panzergrenadier units was supposed to breach the Allied front line, thus opening a path for a second wave (composed of Panzer and Panzergrenadier divisions) that was to penetrate deeply into enemy lines. The battle raged for five days around the Carroceto–Padiglione area before the Germans abandoned the offensive due to heavy losses.

The Fallschirmjäger's role in this counteroffensive was secondary, yet revealing. On the 16th, 'Sturm' FJR 12 attacked British positions held by the 56th Infantry Division at the Moletta Ditch. The 1,381-man regiment breached the British front line with II/FJR 12 taking 113 prisoners, and it succeeded in threatening the road leading to the 'first overpass'. But, since roughly half of its soldiers lacked adequate training and a quarter lacked any combat experience at all, junior officers and NCOs suffered disproportionately high losses. On the 18th the 56th Infantry Division counter-attacked and forced the Fallschirmjäger to retreat. In three days the 'Sturm' Regiment had lost six officers, 40 NCOs and 357 other ranks; II/FJR 12 was left with only four officers.

The Lehr Bataillon suffered a similar fate at Sessano, while 4 Fallschirmjäger Division took heavy losses during the counteroffensive of 27 February to 3 March, even though it only played a secondary role in the operation.

Cassino, March 1944

The Cassino 'Inferno' offered the Fallschirmjäger a perfectly suitable scenario to show their true strengths and capabilities. The town of Cassino was about 500m wide and 1,000m long, it was dominated by a steep hill and faced a river to the east. Hardly more than two battalions could operate in such a narrow area in normal circumstances, and in the case of Cassino circumstances were further worsened by the extensive destruction brought about by persistent artillery fire and aerial bombardment. The terrain was also unsuitable for armoured warfare, which meant that the Fallschirmjäger's lack of heavy weapons did not prove to be a major disadvantage.

In fact, Cassino offered many advantages to the defender. Ruined houses and buildings offered excellent defensive positions, especially since Italian houses were stone-built and often had large cellars that the Fallschirmjäger soon converted into bombproof shelters. The battle became a single-house, single-man fight, where the Allied forces' overwhelming numerical superiority was negated. The Germans also possessed excellent observation posts, which enabled them to spot any enemy penetration and to react appropriately. Heavy weapons were not really needed, in many cases entire companies were halted by snipers or by a single machine-gun position.

A typical scene during the battle for Cassino: ruined houses and debris, providing excellent cover for the defending Fallschirmjäger and a major obstacle for Allied attackers. (Count E.G. Vitetti collection)

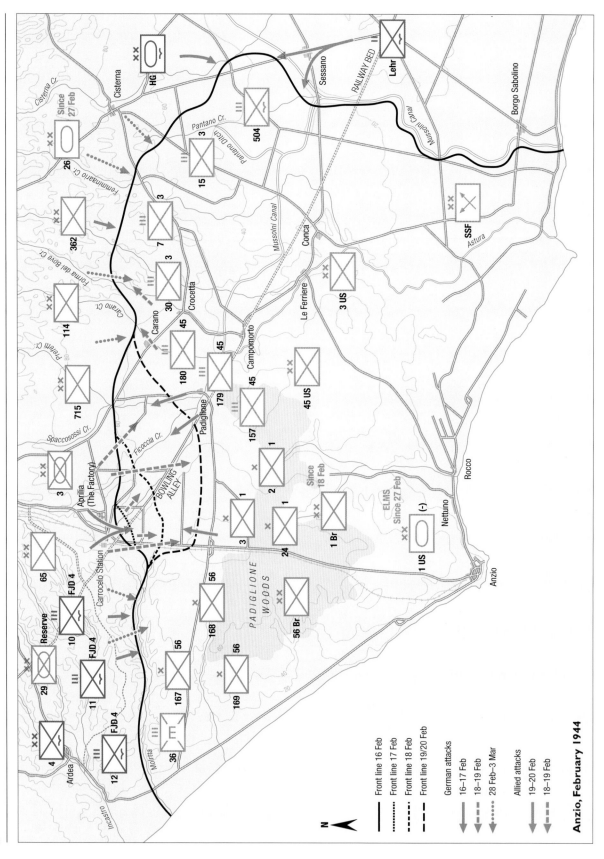

Anzio, February 1944

Front line 16 Feb
Front line 17 Feb
Front line 18 Feb
Front line 19/20 Feb

German attacks
16–17 Feb
18–19 Feb
28 Feb–3 Mar

Allied attacks
19–20 Feb
18–19 Feb

N

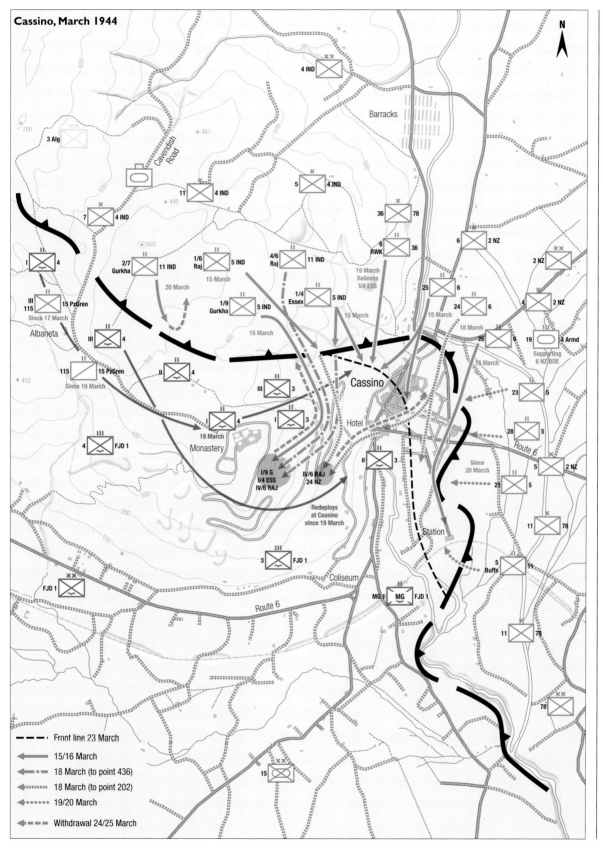

Cassino, March 1944

N

4 IND

Barracks

706
3 Alg

481

Cavendish Road

600

500

11 | 4 IND

445

7 | 4 IND

603

5 | 4 IND

36 | 78

6 RWK

6 | 36

6 | 2 NZ

2 NZ

2/7 Gurkha | 11 IND

1/6 Raj | 5 IND

4/6 Raj | 11 IND

19 March Relieves I/4 ESS

25 | 6

4 | 2 NZ

1 | 4

20 March

15 March

1/4 Essex | 5 IND

24 | 6

4 Armd

19

III 115 | 15 PzGren

Since 17 March

1/9 Gurkha | 5 IND

15 March

15 March

18 March

Supporting 6 NZ BDE

Albaneta

III | 4

26 | 6

15 March

115 | 15 PzGren

Since 19 March

452

III | 3

Cassino

23 | 5

II | 4

I | 4

I | 3

Hotel

28 | 5

Route 6

400

19 March

4 | FJD 1

Monastery

300

I/9 G I/4 ESS IV/6 RAJ

IV/6 RAJ 24 NZ

II | 3

Since 20 March

24 | 5

5 | 2 NZ

200

Redeploys at Cassino since 19 March

11 | 78

100

Station

3 | FJD 1

Coliseum

5 | 11
Buffs

FJD 1

Route 6

MG 1 | MG | FJD 1

11 | 78

78

15

Front line 23 March
15/16 March
18 March (to point 436)
18 March (to point 202)
19/20 March
Withdrawal 24/25 March

German soldiers after their capture, including both ordinary riflemen and Fallschirmjäger, whose apparent attitude is strikingly different. (Count E.G. Vitetti collection)

Inside Cassino, 1944. The two men at the left wear army windproof anoraks in field grey. Three helmet styles are represented here: plain blue-grey, overpainted sandy yellow and one with the splinter camouflage cover.

In spring 1944 1 Fallschirmjäger Division was still largely composed of experienced, battle-hardened soldiers who had been trained to hold their positions at any cost. The Fallschirmjäger were a real elite: selected volunteers who passed through a severe training program and had acquired not only precious battle experience, but also a particular esprit de corps.

The attack against Cassino on 15 March was preceded by a heavy aerial and artillery bombardment. From the north, one New Zealand battalion (supported by tanks) and one Indian battalion attacked Cassino, though they were soon halted by craters and by the furious response from the Fallschirmjäger. To the west of the town two Indian battalions succeeded in getting through the German lines and reached two high positions on the eastern slope of Monastery Hill (points 436 and 202) while hard fighting raged at point 193, which dominated the centre of German resistance: the Hotel Continental. Soon the battle broke up in a series of small engagements, to the Fallschirmjäger's advantage. Their resistance nests could only be reduced to silence by a series of coordinated attacks, which neither the Indians nor the New Zealanders proved capable of doing. Those units at points 436 and 202 were isolated, though the Allies made some progress to the south of Cassino, toward the railroad station.

1 Fallschirmjäger Division also excelled in the classic element of German defensive doctrine: counter-attacking the enemy. I/FJR 4 was relieved and moved to Monastery Hill, launching a counter-attack – soon halted by the defenders – on point 193. On the other hand, III/FJR 4 penetrated in small groups into Cassino to reinforce the strongpoints, thus further strengthening the German defences. Then, the battle was reduced to a fragmented series of small engagements, none of which could bring a real decision. On 24 March the garrisons at points 436 and 202 withdrew, thus putting an end to the third battle of Cassino.

Lessons learned

In spite of their notable successes, after Crete the Fallschirmjäger almost completely failed in the role for which they had been created. Until late 1943, they still were a reasonably powerful force ready to be used for airborne operations However, this force was either wasted in minor airborne operations, or simply used as a kind of elite infantry.

The decay of the German airborne force becomes more starkly obvious when compared with the steady development of both the British and American airborne forces throughout the period, although they too faced many problems and defeats. As the war progressed, German Fallschirmjäger and Allied paratroopers shared the sinilar fate of being used in the infantry role.

Although the purpose and success of many of the World War II airborne operations has been frequently questioned since the end of the war, the same cannot be said of the airborne troops. No matter what Crete, Sicily, Normandy or Arnhem meant to airborne warfare, paratroopers earned distinction as tough and valuable combatants, either dropped by air or marching on foot. Other, non-airborne, units could well have fought battles like Cassino and Bastogne, though the results may well have been very different.

This is the real lesson to be drawn from the employment of airborne forces in World War II, and it is one that the Germans appear to have learnt by late 1943. Although their primary role is to be dropped by air into battle, the real value of airborne units lies in their high-level training, in their capabilities as combatants and in their very special esprit de corps. Qualities that, when combined, make them into exceptional fighting units. Unsurprisingly, Italian paratroopers were the finest units of the entire Italian Army, though they never actually took part in an airborne operation.

Technological developments quickly rendered World War II airborne operations obsolete; gliders disappeared from the battlefield, and the helicopter increasingly replaced the parachute as a tactical means of transporting troops by air. What did not change was the quality of the airborne troops, always the finest combat units. Whether this is the result of their being an all-volunteer highly selected force, or the result of very high training standards is hard to say. Yet, the truth is that this is the main standard feature shared by paratroopers and airborne troops all around the world from World War II to the present day.

And it is ironic, to say the least, that the deterioration of the Fallschirmjäger was caused by the German High Command having discovered such a simple truth. Certainly, although there were a number of reasons behind the dramatic expansion of the Fallschirmtruppen in 1943–44, the major one was that the German wanted to take full advantage of the fighting capabilities of this highly skilled and selected force.

The Mediterranean, which saw the Fallschirmjäger in action in their primary role at Crete, also saw them showing uncommon capabilities in non-airborne operations. The battle of Cassino demonstrates what such elite forces could accomplish – even when their principal role had faded away.

This is perhaps the true reason that paratroopers and other airborne units were retained in the postwar years, even though their original role had been called into question by technological developments. Though not always delivered by air, they stil possess the capabikity of striking hard, suddenly and unexpectedly, so as to throw the enemy completely off balance. Though in a different manner from the one predicted by Benjamin Franklin so long ago.

Bibliography

Ailsby, Christopher, *Sky Warriors: German Paratroopers in Action* (Spellmount, 2000)

Barnett, Correlli (ed.), *Hitler's Generals* (Weidenfeld & Nicolson, 1989)

Blumenson, Martin, *Drive to Rome* (Purnell, 1966)

Böhmler, Rudolf, *Cassino: The Pyrrhic Victory* (Purnell, 1966)

— *From Rome to the Gothic Line* (Purnell, 1966)

— *Retreat to Cassino* (Purnell, 1966)

— *Stalemate at Cassino: The German View* (Purnell, 1966)

Borsarello. J.F. (ed.), *Les Tenues Camouflées de la Deuxieme Guerre Mondiale* (Gazette des uniformes, 1992)

Carver, Field Marshal Lord, *The Imperial War Museum Book of the War in Italy* (Sidgwick & Jackson, 2001)

Churchill, Winston S., *The Second World War*, Vols 4-6 (Cassell, 1950)

Davies, W.J.K., *German Army Handbook 1939–1945* (Arco, 1973)

Davis, Brian L., *German Parachute Forces 1935–45* (Arms & Armour, 1974)

Dell Giudice, Elio e Vittorio, *Atlante delle Uniformi militari italiane dal 1934 ad oggi* (Ermanno Albertelli Editore, 1984)

Ellis, Chris, *7th Flieger Division* (Ian Allan, 2002)

— *The German Army 1933–45* (Ian Allan, 1993)

Ellis, John, *Cassino: The Hollow Victory* (André Deutsch, 1984)

— *The World War II Databook* (Aurum, 1993, 1995)

Ffrench-Blake, Colonel R.L.V., *Victory in Italy* (Purnell, 1966)

Graham, Dominick, *Cassino* (Ballantine, 1971)

Gregory, Barry, and Batchelor, John, *Airborne Warfare 1918–1945* (Phoebus, 1979)

Hibbert, Christopher, *Anzio: Bid for Rome* (Macdonald, 1970)

— *The Rescue of Mussolini* (Purnell, 1966)

Hogg, Ian V., and Weeks, John, *Military Small Arms of the 20th Century* (Arms & Armour, 1977)

Jackson, W.G.F., *The Battle for Rome* (Batsford, 1969)

Kemp, Peter, *Sicily: The Conquest* (Purnell, 1966)

Kesselring, Albert, *Memoirs* (Kimber, 1953)

Kühn, Volkmar, *Deutsche Fallschirmjäger im Zweiten Weltkrieg* (5th edn) (Motorbuch, 1985)

— *Mit Rommel in die Wüste* (Motorbuch, 1975)

Lucas, James, *German Army Handbook 1939–1945* (Sutton, 1998)

— *Storming Eagles: German Airborne Forces in World War Two* (Arms & Armour, 1988)

Mitcham, Samuel W., *Hitler's Legions* (Leo Cooper, 1985)

Nafziger, George F., *The German Order of Battle: Panzers and Artillery in World War II and Infantry in World War II* (Greenhill Books, 1999, 2000)

— *Waffen SS and Other Units in World War II* (Combined Publishing, 2001)

Neillands, Robin, *Eighth Army* (John Murray, 2004)

Orgill, Douglas, *Italy: The Autumn Battles* (Purnell, 1966)

— *Stalemate on the Gothic Line* (Purnell, 1966)

Packer, Edwin, *Hard Lesson in the Aegean (Dodecanese, September–November 1943)* (Purnell, 1966)

Parker, Matthew, *Monte Cassino* (Headline, 2003)

Piekalkiewicz, J., *Cassino: Anatomy of a Battle* (Orbis, 1980)

Pöppel, Martin, *Heaven and Hell: The War Diary of a German Paratrooper* (Spellmount, 1988)

Price, Dr Alfred, *The Luftwaffe Data Book* (Greenhill Books, 1997)

Quarrie, Bruce, *Airborne Assault* (Patrick Stephens, 1991)

— *Fallschirmjäger* (Osprey, 2001)

— *Fallschirmpanzerdivision 'Hermann Göring'* (Osprey, 1978)

— *German Airborne Divisions Blitzkrieg 1940–41* (Osprey, 2004)

— *German Airborne Troops 1939–45* (Osprey, 1983)

— *German Paras in the Med* (Patrick Stephens, 1979)

Ramcke, Bernhard, *Vom Schiffszungen zum Fallschirmjäger General* (Verlag die Wehrmacht, 1943)

Rhodes, Anthony, *The Fall of Mussolini* (Purnell, 1966)

— *Sicily: The Prelude and the Assault* (Purnell, 1966)

Seaton, Albert, *The German Army 1939–1945* (Weidenfeld & Nicolson, 1982)

Senger und Etterlin, Frido von, *Neither Fear Nor Hope* (Presidio, 1989)

Smith, J.R., Kay, Anthony, & Creek, E.J., *German Aircraft of the Second World War* (Putnam, 1972)

Strawson, Brigadier John, *The Battle for North Africa* (Ace Books, 1969)

Trevelyan, Raleigh, *Anzio – Blast and Counterblast* (Purnell, 1966)

— *Anzio: The Lull* (Purnell, 1966)

— *Rome '44* (Secker & Warburg, 1981)

Glossary

Notes: (1) Words almost identical in English have not been included, e.g., Artillerie/Artigliera, Bataillon/Battaglione, Korps/Corpo. (2) Italian does not capitalize ranks, e.g. maggiore (Major), but I have done so for the convenience of English-speaking readers.

Abbreviations

AFV Armoured fighting vehicle

BAR Browning automatic rifle

C/C Controcarri

Cdo Comando

Cp Compagnia

C3 Italian codename for proposed invasion of Malta in 1942

DPM Disruptive pattern material (camouflage)

FAR Fallschirm-Artillerie Regiment

Feldfu Feldfunkgerät, field radio equipment

FJR Fallschirmjäger Regiment

Flak Flugzeug-Abwehr Kanone, anti-aircraft (gun)

Ftr Fanteria

Fuspr Funksprech, voice radio, R/T

Gr Gruppo

GrW Granatewerfer, 'grenade thrower', ie. mortar

(GS) Grossraumlastensegler, great room cargo glider, Me 321

hmg heavy machine gun

IR Infanterie Regiment

Kdo Kommando

KG Kampfgruppe, Bomber Group, equivalent to RAF Wing

lG leichte Geschütz, light gun

LLStR Luftlande-Sturm Regiment, Airlanding Assault Regiment

lmg light machine gun

MAS MTB

MG Maschinengewehr, machine gun

MKb Maschinenkarabiner, machine carbine

MP Maschinenpistole, machine pistol (smg) or Military Police

OK Oberkommando, High Command

   -H des Heeres, of the Army

   -L der Luftwaffe, of the Air Force

   -W der Wehrmacht, of the armed forces

PaK Panzerabwehr Kanone, anti-tank gun

Par Paracacadutisti

PJK Panzerjäger Kanone, tank-hunter gun

POW prisoner of aar

Pz Panzer, armour, tank

   -AOK Panzerarmee Oberkommando, tank army high command

RATO Rocket assisted take-off

Rep Reparto

RSHA Reichssicherheitshauptamt, Reich Security Head Office (SS)

RLM Reichsluftfahrtministerium, German Air Transport Ministry

RPzB Racketenpanzerbüchse, rocket anti-tank rifle

RSI Repubblica Sociale Italiana, Italian Social Republic, breakaway fascist 'government' after the armistice

SD Sicherheitsdienst, Security Service (SS)

Sez Sezione

Sipo Sicherheitspolizei, Security Police (SS)

smg sub-machine gun

sPzB schwere Panzerbüchse, heavy anti-tank rifle

SS Schutzstaffel, Protection Squadron

StG Sturmgewehr, assault rifle

WGr Wurfgranate, 'throw grenade', i.e. rocket projector

zbV zur besonderen Verwendungs, for special disposal

Abteilung Detachment, frequently used to describe a battalion-sized unit

Abwehr Defence, the principal OKW intelligence service

Alpini Mountain troops

Ardito(*pl-* i) Literally, daring or bold; in context, volunteer (German Freiwillige)

Armata An army, as distinct from the Army

Aufklärungs Reconnaissance

Ausbildungs 'Building', training

Barbarossa Codename for German invasion of Russia in 1941

Befehlshaber Commander-in-Chief

Bewärungs Probationary

Brillianten Diamonds (to Ritterkreuz)

Carabinieri Armed police (the Italian 'Senior Service')

Commando Supremo Italian High Command

Comunicazioni Signals

Contraereo Anti-aircraft

Controcarri Anti-tank

Corazzato Armoured

Crusader British codename for December 1941 offensive in Africa

d'Aviosbarco Airlanding

Decima Tenth

Distruttori Destroyer, e.g, 'arditi distruttori', daring destroyers

Eichenlaub Oakleaves (to Ritterkreuz)

Ersatz Replacement, substitute

Esercito The Army, as distinct from an army

Esplorante Reconnaissance

Fall Gelb (Case Yellow) Codename for 1940 offensive in the west

Fallschirm Parachute

   -jäger (*no pl*) Paratroop(s)

   -schützenabzeichen Paratroop Badge, 'Wings'

Fanteria Infantry

Fanti dell'Aria Airborne infantry

Flieger Flying, usually translated as Airborne

Freikorps Free Corps

Führer Leader

   -hauptquartier Hitler's headquarters

Funk Radio

Gebirgsjäger Mountain troop(s)

Genio Engineers

Gerät Equipment

Geschwader Wing, equivalent of RAF/USAAF Group

Grün Teufel Green Devil, nickname for the Fallschirmjäger

Gruppo (*pl* -i) Group(s), used for artillery battalions and sometimes like German Abteilung to denote other battalion-size units

Guastatori Saboteurs (assault engineers)

Heer The German Army

Heeresleitung (Department of) Army Direction

Herbstnebel (Autumn Mist) Codename for Ardennes offensive in December 1944

Herkules (Hercules) Codename for proposed invasion of Malta in 1942

Husky Allied codename for invasion of Sicily in 1943

Jagdverbände Hunting Band, SS anti-partisan force

Kampfgruppe (a) Battlegroup, a formation of indeterminate size and composition; (b) Bomber Group

Kommandobefehl Commando Order

kurz, kurzer short, shorter

Landespolizei Provincial Police

Lastensegler Cargo glider

Lightfoot Codename for British Alamein counter-offensive in October 1942

Luftflotte Air Fleet

Luftlande Airlanding

Luftwaffe German Air Force after 1935

Luftwaffen-Feld Luftwaffe Field (Division, etc)

   -jäger Air Force light infantry

Maresciallo Marshal

   -dell'Aria Air Marshal

Mas Motor torpedo boat

Maschinen (of machine)

   -gewehr (MG) Machine gun

   -karabiner (MKb) Machine carbine

   -pistole (MP) Machine pistol

Matrose Naval rating, ordinary seaman

Merkur (Mercury) Codename for the invasion of Crete in 1941

Mincemeat British codename for deception operation in 1943

Mortai Mortar

Motociclisti Motorcyle-mounted infantry

Nachrichten Signals

Nachschub Supply

Nuotatori Swimmer

Oberbefehlshaber Supreme Commander-in-Chief

Panzerfaust 'Armour fist': (1) Hollow-charge anti-tank weapon; (2) codename for operation in Hungary to kidnap Admiral Horthy's son

Panzerschreck 'Armour battleaxe', 8.8cm RPzB54, equivalent of bazooka

Paracadutisti Parachutists

Pionier (*pl* –e) Combat engineer(s)

Püppchen 'Little doll', RPzB54 on two-wheel carriage

Racketenwerfer Rocket projector

Raggruppamento Battlegroup

Regia Aeronautica Royal (Italian) Air Force

Regia Marina Royal (Italian) Navy

Regio Esercito Royal (Italian) Army

Reparto Department

Ritterkreuz Knight's Cross

Rößelsprung (Knight's Move) Codename for operation to capture Tito in 1944

Sanità (It), **Sanitäts** (Ger) Medical

Schleppgruppe Tow Group for gliders

Schwerten Swords (to Ritterkreuz)

Sëelowe (Sealion) Codename for proposed invasion of England in 1940

Servizi Services

Sezione Section

Spreng High explosive

Stab Staff

Standarte SS equivalent of regiment

Stato Maggiore Chief of staff

Sturm Storm, assault

Süd South

Sussistenza Supply

Tagesbefehl Order of the Day

Torch Allied codename for invasion of French north-west Africa in 1942

Unternehmen Undertaking, operation

Wehrmacht Armed forces excluding the Waffen-SS

Zug (*pl* Züge) Platoon(s)

Index